THE
RETURN
OF
BURKE
AND
HARE

A Musical Comedy
by Raymond Burke

dualchas
Glasgow

D1347943

First published in 1994
by dualchas
1/R, 21 Garturk St, Glasgow

Text Copyright © 1991 Raymond Burke
Music & Lyrics Copyright © 1991 Raymond Burke
Introduction Copyright © 1994 Owen Dudley Edwards
ISBN 0 9521418 3 3 The Return of Burke and Hare
(Paperback)

British Library Cataloguing in Publication Data
A Catalogue Record for this book is available from the
British Library.

Printed by Clydeside Press, 37 High Street, Glasgow.

DEDICATED TO
Paul Burke
1960 - 1994

Contents

Introduction

by Owen Dudley Edwards

When a man named Raymond Burke writes a musical comedy about a man named William Burke, what call (as they would say in my mother's native Cork) have I to intrude an introduction? Nor does Raymond Burke take coy refuge in pleas of 'no relation' : to the contrary, he told the Edinburgh Festival press in August 1991 before the play's presentation at the Gilded Balloon on the Edinburgh Cowgate (along which the original Burke and Hare had passed with many a corpse in 1828) that he himself may very well be a descendant of the famous murderer of fifteen persons for medical dissection. William Burke left a wife and family in Ireland before coming to Scotland in 1818 to work on the Union Canal, where he met and fell in love with Helen MacDougal. Nothing is known of the fate of his descendants.

Of this last point I was made all too clearly if charmingly aware by Her Excellency the President of the Republic of Ireland, Dr Mary Robinson, when she kindly accepted a copy of my own play *Hare and Burke* in mid-July 1994. The President smiled that the gift was most appropriate, in that her maiden name was Burke: in addition to the many other admirable ways in which she represents the best qualities of her countryfolk, Mary Robinson has a peculiarly elegant prowess in obtaining the last laugh.

I suppose my claim to introduce is that I have written *Hare and Burke* , and, for that matter, *Burke and Hare* , the latter a history, the former an attempt to find through theatre the parts of the story history could not reach (how

5

Hare —or, as I believe, Margaret Hare— succeeded in manoeuvring the Lord Advocate so as to win immunity for 16 murders; and how Burke managed to ensure that his defence and Helen MacDougal's were coordinated so that, while he was found Guilty, the charge against her was Not Proven (quite rightly: she seems to have known nothing of the murders, save the last one, and certainly did not help in that although she did try to conceal it.). But surely this makes me Mr Raymond Burke's adversary. I sought to prove in history and drama that while William Burke was indeed a multi-murderer, he was otherwise a man of honour and dignity and even humanity, who was horribly racked by conscience for his hideous deeds, where Mr Raymond Burke (with a possible descendant's assurance) portrays an utterly amoral if genial villain. In fact, in *The Return of Burke and Hare*, it is Hare who shows signs of conscience by seeing a reanimated victim of whom Burke remains ignorant and Dr Knox makes short work.

Even physically, Burke and Hare were reversed in the play as presented under Raymond Burke's direction. All witnesses confirm that the original Hare was a tall, gangling, ghastly, and (in Sir Walter Scott's words) "a most hideous wretch .... if he was not some depraved villain, Nature did not write with a legible hand". *The Return of Burke and Hare* produced a diminutive, attractive, even lovable Hare. Hugh Larkin made him an entrancing, capering elf, whose escape from justice seemed less a legal solecism than an indulgence to be accorded to a mischievous Blytonian brownie. Raymond Burke has the pleasure of simultaneous possession and consumption of his cake here: his Hare is equally guilty with Burke and yet in Hugh Larkin's magic hands the audience's sympathies homologate the Crown's filthy bargain. We have seen Ron Moody transform Dickens' Fagin into everybody's favourite old rascal in the musical *Oliver* : and the citation is appropriate since *Oliver Twist*, written less than a decade after the Burke and Hare murders, may well have drawn on them (although with Fagin reflecting the more diplomatic and intellectual Burke where Bill Sikes exhibited the brutality and misanthropy of the actual Hare). And as Hugh Douglas shows in his informative if crudely dehumanising *Burke and Hare* (1973), nineteenth-century popular stage shows on Burke and Hare sometimes made a comic character of Hare. It may be doubted if the performances approach Hugh Larkin's.

On the other hand, where the original William Burke was 5 foot 6 inches (which I confirm from measurement of his skeleton) Raymond Burke cast him as a dominating six footer, menacing, captivating, brutal and in command, never more so than when undertaking the part himself. In a sense the close of the play with Burke playing Burke finally captured in his own trap and enmeshed in his own play, gives an even more subtle example of cake possession-and-consumption. Theatrically, the duo worked to perfection, all the more when joined by Knox, the little figure of Hare admirably setting off the two big ones in the triumphant leaps around the circle to the thunderous strains of "*Transplant Surgery's What It's All About*". I can personally testify that the sound of percussion and jumping feet to that tune has haunted me for the last three years.

But why should I applaud and evangelise work traducing the memory of William Burke, whose name I have sought to defend for the last 14 years?

Firstly, the artistic quality of a play must often be independent of its historical truth. We acknowledge *Macbeth* one of the greatest tragedies ever written: it is also an appalling cascade of defamation at the expense of a noble ruler whose chief blemish in the eyes of his subjects was his generosity. I was a great admirer of the *Burke and Hare* staged at the Edinburgh Festival Fringe (a year or so before *The Return of Burke and Hare*) by Hillhead Academy of Aberdeen, and its William Burke was much nastier than Raymond Burke's, particularly at the brilliantly dramatic moment when he realises that Daft Jamie Wilson was not the idiot he appeared but a boy too clever to be articulate and the only person to have detected the murders: and so the boy detective is murdered himself. It was as though the Queen of Hearts had really chopped off Alice's head; and made for excellent, if chilling, theatre.

But in any case Raymond Burke is in a perfect position to play any pranks he may please on the original story: for *The Return of Burke and Hare* is set in the present. Any pieces of the actual events of 1828 are simple building materials for Raymond Burke: so Nell MacDougal may be guilty, and the original poverty-stricken Grays brought back as wealthy English ("Simon" and "Susan"), and William Burke given free tenancy at the Hare hotel by William instead of Margaret Hare. Raymond Burke tells what is chiefly a story of his own creation, and for all the brilliance of his use of musical comedy, and its hilarity as text and as theatre he has a grim moral to point with it. He is not , in fact, the descendant of William Burke so much as of Brendan Behan and Joe Orton (whose identification with ancestry is Ortonian enough in its humour). Admittedly, the original William Burke had rather a nice line in black humour, as when he remarked in his last days that Dr Robert Knox still owed him for the last corpse, and he could do with another pair of trousers for his forthcoming public appearance (meaning on the gallows). But the resolution with which Raymond Burke will drive his dialogue through scarifyingly shallow jokes only to emerge unscathed leaving his audience helpless with angry laughter, has nothing to equal it since Behan's *The Hostage*. Orton may offer more profound absurdities, more complex and intricate a web of mystification in which logic inverts itself into mind-boggling nonsense: but Orton lacks as obvious a target as Behan or Raymond Burke have set themselves. We may all be at war against cliché or pomposity or petty tyranny, but the cutting edge of the blackest humour is honed in the more personal war, the more specific crusade. Behan had the central agenda of indicting political ideology when it sacrifices human nature. And Raymond Burke, at the heart of his musical comedy, heavy sound and all, is bluntly telling us that wealth may now command murder so that poverty can supply its anatomical deficiencies.

So, ironically, Raymond Burke's essentially anti-historical play, which deliberately removes historical events and persons from their times and contexts, makes a brilliant deduction from a historical crisis of the past. We know that the poor rioted against the doctors and anatomical dissection on the ground that the diseases of the rich were being cured by murders of the poor whose bodies supplied the basis of research. Riots during the cholera epidemic of 1831-32 declaimed that cry. It may have been unjust : arguably the doctors of 1828-32 had no clear notion of what they would find from their anatomical research, and the beneficiaries of any cures they discovered might have been rich and poor alike. Sir Walter Scott saw a want of humanity in the zeal for science as lying at the heart of the doctors' indifference to the possibility of murder to produce subjects: "The pursuers of physical studies inflict tortures on the lower animals of creation, and at length come to rub shoulders with the West Port" he wrote to Maria Edgeworth on 4th February 1829 a week after Burke's execution (Burke and Hare had carried out their murders in that quarter of Edinburgh). "*Here* is a doctor who is able to take down the whole clockwork of the human frame, and may in time find some way of repairing and putting it together again; and *there* is Burke with the body [of his] murdered countrywoman on his back, and her blood on his hands, asking his price from the learned carcass-butcher." But Raymond Burke has a strong case that the class exploitation, whether present or not in the medical researches of 1828, has all too likely a relevance to the world of the 1990's. We are today growing into new class polarisation, and the new primacy given to Wealth takes its privileges the more ruthlessly through having violated social compacts of past generations. Medicine which fifty years ago was at the service of all, is today being forced more and more back into a two-tier system. To posit a world in which expensive transplants go only to persons who will pay for them ,and are achieved by murder of persons who cannot guard against them, is to envisage a logical future for the Thatcherite state. The original Burke-Hare violation of laws of hospitality, exploitation of one's own ethnic and economic group, recognition of a logical arena in which to pioneer new business enterprise based on expertise in the people destined for destruction

— are very obvious traditions to be reinvoked in our increasingly brazen worship of the business culture.

Mr Raymond Burke wants us to enjoy his play, to laugh, to sing, to dance, all of which he makes it very easy for us to do. But the high comedy reaches its peak in the audience's sense of auctorial anger behind the laughter, in the lash of satire whistling behind the easy smack of lampoon. *The Return of Burke and Hare* is a work of fine wit, song and pace, and a masterly plucking of comedy from the heart of tragedy: but it is comedy that is all the stronger for having the divine rage against human cruelty and destructiveness which first gave Comedy wings in the drama of Aristophanes.

Department of History
University of Edinburgh
September 1994

Special thanks to
Owen Dudley Edwards, Tommy Fowler, Ross Stenhouse,
The Mad Millers, Alasdair Smith, Gordon Munro,
Peter Thomson, Andy Arnold, Stevie Burns,
E.K. Comm. Ed., The Key, Wee Stan, Gillian, Kevin,
Stuart Perry, Gary Christie, The Kilby...
and the original Burke and Hare, without whom this work would
have been total fiction.

Author's Notes

When I began writing this play, my intention was to create a Music Hall / Dickensian comedy following the actual story of Burke and Hare, set in the early nineteenth century and jazzed up somewhat with a song or two. But on closer comparison of their morals with today's 'all-right jack' ethics, it became obvious that the bodysnatchers would find a more fitting home, and voracious market, in our own 'modern' ideological surroundings. Hence- The 'Return' of Burke and Hare, performed in top hats and tails to portray a 'Hammer House of Horror' feel, but set in the near future to present the Thatcherite legacy of tomorrow... William Burke, William Hare and friends have thus, further traversed the journey immortal. All of the main characters appearing in the play are taken from the history books, by name, if not by nature, and the plot follows the adventure, justification and betrayal in Burke and Hare's true story. Their names and deeds have survived the test of time far better than those of their judges, rivals and executioners, and will almost certainly outlast those of both you and I. But this is purely entertainment and not a history lesson, so read on, sing along and —

— have a nice death!

Raymond Burke 1994

The return of Burke and Hare was first presented at the East Kilbride Village Theatre on 17th April 1991 by the KYBO theatre company, with the following cast:

HARE .... Hugh Larkin
MAGGIE .... Helen Barr
BURKE .... Gary Cross
NELL .... Mari Steven
UNDERTAKER 1, POLICEMAN .... Richard McLean
UNDERTAKER 2, JAMIE, CONSTABLE OUTSIDE .... Andrew Wright
MR GRAY .... Fraser Cross
ABIGAIL .... Pauline Marshall
Dr KNOX .... Tam Quinn
Mrs GRAY .... Joanne Nimmo
JUDGE RAMBO PICKLES .... Gerry McHugh
PROSTITUTE .... Kate Cetan
MAN IN CRUTCHES, Mr GRAY II .... John Martin
TRAMP .... Raymond Burke

Directed by Raymond Burke

The same production subsequently transferred to the Gilded Balloon, Edinburgh, as part of the Edinburgh Festival Fringe, where it opened on 9th August 1991, with the following cast:

HARE .... Hugh Larkin
MAGGIE .... Julie McCahill
BURKE .... Raymond Burke
NELL .... Mari Steven
UNDERTAKER 1, POLICEMAN .... Richard McLean
UNDERTAKER 2, Dr KNOX,
CONSTABLE OUTSIDE, MAN IN CRUTCHES .... Craig Allan
Mr GRAY .... Fraser Cross
JAMIE, Mr GRAY II .... Stevie Foster
Mrs GRAY, PROSTITUTE .... Kate Cetan
ABIGAIL, JUDGE RAMBO PICKLES .... Gerry McHugh
TRAMP .... Kevin Everett

Directed by Raymond Burke and Gerry McHugh

The 'BODYSNATCHING BAND' was:

Gerry McHugh .... Piano, Guitar and Musical Direction
Tam Graham .... Lead Guitar
Simon McBain .... Bass (E.K.)
Alex Harris .... Bass (Edin.)
Alan Platt .... Drums

Choreography .... Kate Cetan

THE RETURN OF BURKE AND HARE

SCENE ONE

Music-Overture and BURKE and HARE Theme.

(*Hares Hotel. There is a small bar upstage right, a table and three chairs downstage of bar, an alcove with an open coffin set inside it stage left. Door to kitchen downstage right. Door to street centrestage at back and door to bedrooms upstage left at top of small flight of stairs . There are various glasses and empty bottles lying around from the previous nights festivities. HARE enters from upstairs, lifts used glass from bar and pours in the few remaining drops from a whisky bottle. He drinks it, looks at the empty glass looks at the coffin weighs the glass and is about to throw it when MAGGIE enters from the kitchen.*)

MAGGIE: And another thing! You can take Clint Skint with you and go and look for some work. The Burkes are the only long term guests that we've got and you invited them to stay here for nothing. And don't you tell him about this, you know what he's like he could talk a taxi driver into a short cut.

HARE: But Maggie....

MAGGIE: Just tell him that his rent's going up from bugger all to bugger me!

HARE: That's inflation for you.

MAGGIE: This hotel's going out of business, you know. Aye that's what you need, work, real work, hard work, one of those good old fashioned factory jobs that'll give you cancer when you're older, a job that keeps you sweating twelve hours a day, toiling seven days a week and coughing up blood for twenty years after you retire.

HARE: And what if I say no?

MAGGIE: The hotel belongs to me, remember. You can't, or you'll end up crawling the streets with your pals. So, you'd better start making some money, somehow, soon.

(*MAGGIE exits to kitchen*)

HARE: Oh, shut up! You're like a broken record. Round and cracked!

(*He goes behind the bar*)

And the only useful bit's the hole.

(*MAGGIE enters behind him and hits him with a tray and exits. HARE stands up, gets a glass and starts to search around looking for a drink but finding only empty bottles. BURKE enters from upstairs.*)

BURKE: Good idea Willie, I'll have one of the same.

(*He walks towards Donald's coffin*)

Are you feeling any better this morning then Donald? No? I think he's faking it to avoid Maggies breakfast.

HARE: I don't know what you're so cheerful about. C'mere and help me find some whisky. It can't be finished, somebody must've planked it.

BURKE: Excuse me Donald.

(Reaches into coffin and searches about. Pulls out bottle of whisky.)

Tah nah! There we go!

HARE: So, that's what you're up so early for. Frightened that they take the whisky away with him?

BURKE: That would be ironic, teetotal all of his life and gets a knock back from heaven for trying to sneak in with a carry out. Do you think we should stick the lid on?

HARE: No. Don't bother, the undertakers get paid for doing that. I'm not wasting any more time on him, he's cost me a fortune already. That's what Maggie was just moaning about, me letting him stay here for nothing until he got his pension.

BURKE: Couldn't you collect it since by rights it's yours?

HARE: No, there's nothing I can do now, I'm flogging a dead horse trying to get cash out of that old shite.

BURKE: That might not be such a bad idea.

HARE: What?

BURKE: Flogging a dead horse.

HARE: What?

BURKE: Flogging as in selling and dead horse as in old shite.

HARE: What?

BURKE: Listen, last week I was having a drink with this doctor, Knox was his name, and he was telling me about the 1989 body shortage.

HARE: Body shortage?

BURKE: Don't tell me you've never heard of the 1989 body shortage!

HARE: You're making this up aren't you?

BURKE: No! Look, have you got any donor cards?

HARE: What's that got to do with it?

BURKE: Have you?

HARE: No danger, I don't want anybody footering about inside me when I'm dead.

BURKE: There you go then, that's what most people say.

HARE: I don't blame them.

BURKE: Nor do I. So, the doctors were desperate for cadavers, it was murder, well not murder exactly, but it was close. What they used to do was buy the corpses from their unscrupulous relatives.

HARE: The things some people do for money! How much did they get?

BURKE: There was a minute turnover of donor cards and folk who had willed themselves to medical research, but not nearly enough. So the doctors took risks, and more importantly, still do. Nobody seems to want to get chopped up and plopped into little jars nowadays. (*To Donald*) Do they? No, they all want to fly to heaven in a glorious cloud of smoke! Meanwhile what is now a teaspoonful of ash could have taken some poor bastard off of a kidney machine. And don't forget, you and I could have made some extra money out of the spare bits.

HARE: Spare bits?

BURKE: The rest of the body, hearts, eyes, liver, lungs maybe, everything you can transplant.

HARE: Bollocks!

BURKE: Probably, but I don't fancy walking about wearing somebody else's!

HARE: If you mean that we should do the same thing with him, we can't. The Undertakers are on their way here, right now.

BURKE: Well, if we put him back up in his room and nail the lid on, nobody will know he's missing. Then in half an hour, ploppety plop, six feet below and who's to know?

HARE: We'll have to get a move on.

BURKE: Move?

HARE: On!

BURKE: Right give me a hand, I'll take him
upstairs you put something else into the
coffin to give it weight and get the lid on.

(*BURKE lifts Donald over his shoulder and exits
upstairs.*)

HARE: What will I..... ? Typical, put something
into the coffin...

(*He looks around for something heavy, tests weight
of phone, puts it down, lifts empty bottle.*)

No, it might have to burn.

(*Puts a beermat in and lifts one end*)

Still needs a wee bit more.... hold it.

(*He opens the kitchen door and shouts through*)

Maggie! Is he getting burnt?... I mean is
Donald getting buried or cremated?

MAGGIE: *(Off)* What do you want to know that
for? Are they here?

HARE: No, I just wondered...

MAGGIE: I told you last night, there's a family
plot with all his ancestors in it, so there
must have been some money somewhere
along the line. I'll tell you this William Hare
...

(Her voice fades as he lets the door close)

HARE: Good, it doesn't need to burn then...

*(He exits through front door, MAGGIE enters with
plate and a fish slice.)*

MAGGIE: And another thing, you can stop
worrying about Donald and go and... where
is he? Are you hiding.... ?

*(She leaves plate and exits to kitchen again. HARE
enters carrying a large rock)*

HARE: That'll do you!

(Puts rock in coffin, tests weight.)

Just a touch more...

*(He sees his breakfast and tips it into the coffin,
        puts the lid on top, goes behind the bar to
        get hammer and nails, BURKE enters)*

BURKE: Are you nearly finished? *(Tests weight)*
    That's not bad. What's in it?

HARE: Just a lot of old crap. *(Starts to nail lid
    down)*

BURKE: That'll be good for the rhubarb in the
    cemetery.

(MAGGIE enters)

MAGGIE: So you're up then?

BURKE: No, I'm still in my bed, this is me
    sleepwalking.

MAGGIE: How's Nell feeling this morning?

BURKE: She'll recover in a year or two.

HARE: *(Hitting thumb)* Arghhh!

BURKE: Here, give me that.

MAGGIE: What are you doing now?

BURKE: I'm making a coffee table for a family of midgets.

MAGGIE: Well stop it!

BURKE: If Nell gets a look at his coupon she'll explode again, she's been up all night artexing the bedroom carpet.

MAGGIE: The undertakers will do that when they get here.

HARE: What, artex the bedroom carpet?

MAGGIE: If you're that bored, why don't you go and get a job of your own?

BURKE: I'm not bored. And if I was bored, I wouldn't be that bored.

MAGGIE: Did you get your breakfast Willie?

HARE: Aye, magic. Thanks, mmm...

MAGGIE: You must've been hungry! (*Looking at empty plate*)

HARE: Aye, it filled a hole.

(*BURKE puts last nail in*)

BURKE: That'll keep the worms out!(*NELL enters*) Morning Nell, did you finish your decorating?

NELL: What's all the banging about? I thought they were taking him away.

MAGGIE: Billy was just putting him out of sight.

NELL: Well, I wish you would stop banging when I'm in my bed. (*She sits at table*)

HARE: I bet you didn't say that last night! (*MAGGIE slaps him*)

BURKE: Willie! Come on we've got some business to attend to. See you when I get back Nell. (*Sneaks up behind her and shouts*) Cheerio!! Ha ha! (*Exits*)

HARE: We're er... going down the Job Centre.

(*Exits*)

NELL: Job Centre? Do they know where it is?

MAGGIE: I don't think so, you've a better chance of seeing Prince Phillip and the Queen applying for a job. Do you fancy some grub?

NELL: No way.

MAGGIE: Some party,wasn't it? (*Sits*) Sorry, wake. There's not much difference between a wake and a party.

NELL: There's not much difference between a wake and a sleep in here. Now I know what Donald feels like.

MAGGIE: There'll be no partying tonight, the brewery's refused to deliver and the pumps are dry. I've seen more bevy at an A.A. meeting in Saudi Arabia.

NELL: Good, I need a night off.

MAGGIE: Are you sure you're not hungry?

NELL: I suppose I'd better try and keep something down. (*There is a confident knock on the door*) Who'll that be? Look at the state of me. It could be a new guest.

MAGGIE: No chance, it'll be the Undertakers to take the last one away. Do us a favour Nell, get rid of them as fast as you can and I'll fix you some breakfast.

(*MAGGIE exits into kitchen. NELL opens front door. UNDERTAKERS enter in pink boiler suits carrying clipboards*)

UNDERTAKERS 1&2: UNDERTAKERS!

NELL: Come in gentlemen, we didn't expect you so early.

UNDERTAKER 1: You're very lucky madam, there's a lot of lateness in this trade.

UNDERTAKER 2: 147! (*Ticking notes on clipboard*)

UT1: That's why we're always so prompt, the

customers are sick to death of it.

UT2: 148!

NELL: Er... well, here he is, number 148.

UT2: He's not number 148.

NELL: But he just said 148.

UT1: Oh, it's a little game we undertakers play. We count how many times people mention death...

UT2: Or dying.

UT1:... or dying, in everyday conversation, and we add it up at the end of the week!

UT2: I've won it for the past fortnight!

NELL: It sounds a bit silly to me.

UT1: Well, it helps the time pass away.

UT2: 149!

UT1: What?

UT2: Pass away!

UT1: Nice one! So, this is Mr Macpherson.
       (*Reading and ticking clipboard*) Natural
       causes, death certificate, embalmed, to be
       buried in family plot, all right for some
       people, insurance company coffin with
       plastic brass-look handles... okay! You sign
       here... and here.... thank you. Here's your
       receipt, and the lids on already!

UT2: Insurance company coffin? Lucky it fits.

NELL: Aye, somebody's making a killing.

UT1&2: 150!

NELL: If you're finished would you take it and
        leave.

UT1: Only a bit of fun while we're doing our job.

NELL: You're not doing it very well.

UT2: We are professionals. Do you know I had to
        go to university?

UT1: For his goners degree.

UT2: There was a lot of stiff competition.

UT1: It wasn't easy being buried in his books for years.

NELL: Will you be quiet! Undertakers are supposed to be serene and depressing not playing games and having a giggle.

UT2: But we use the modern approach.

UT1: Funerals shouldn't be sad..

UT2: Dull..

UT1: Boring...

UT2: Dull...

UT1: Miserable...

UT2: Dull...

UT1: Lamenting and...

UT2: Dullllll.

UT1: They should be more...

UT1&2: Cheerful!

UT1: You should realise that the day you die is the last chance you'll ever get to have a nice time.

UT2: So, we don't say cheerio, goodbye or au-revoir...

UT1: But- Have a nice death!

NELL: Have a nice death?

UT2: Yes- Have a nice death!

Music-HAVE A NICE DEATH

Chorus
UT1&2:
Have a nice death, have a nice death,
You started out with nothing and you've nothing less.
Have a nice death, have a nice death,
All you did was eat and sleep and waste your breath.

Verse 1
UT1: You lived your life so lonely, you never had a friend.
UT2: No one to cry a tear for you when coming to the end.
UT1&2: You're feeling sorry for yourself don't feel so sorry for yourself.
UT1: You lived your life in misery, you never raised a smile.
UT2: You'd like to have been happy but you never had the style.

| UT1&2: | You're feeling sorry for yourself don't feel so sorry for yourself.
You're feeling sorry for yourself, stop feeling sorry for yourself. |

Chorus

| UT1&2: | Have a nice death, have a nice death,
You started out with nothing and you've nothing less.
Have a nice death, have a nice death,
All you did was eat and sleep and waste your breath. |

Verse 2

UT1:	We're pleasantly informal when we use the formalin.
UT2:	We all rehearse to drive the hearse to stuff your body in.
UT1&2:	You're feeling sorry for yourself don't feel so sorry for yourself.
UT1:	We'll make your funeral happier, we'll sing and tell you jokes.
UT2:	We'll dance with all your relatives and entertain your folks.
UT1&2:	You're feeling sorry for yourself don't feel so sorry for yourself. You're feeling sorry for yourself, stop feeling sorry for yourself.

Middle bit

| UT1&2: | Everybody's going to do it some day,
But the people should be smiling when we carry them away.
They seem to want the family there and all their friends in tears,
Dead flowers for memories in all the coming years. |

Chorus

| UT1&2: | Have a nice death, have a nice death,
You started out with nothing and you've nothing less.
Have a nice death, have a nice death,
All you did was eat and sleep and waste your breath. |

Verse 3

UT1:	When you reminisce in heaven you can flap your wings with joy.
UT2:	Pluck your harp in melody, you're such a lucky boy.
UT1&2:	You're feeling sorry for yourself don't feel so sorry for yourself.
UT1:	Your send off was magnificent the day you disappeared.
UT2:	We plopped your coffin in the ground and everybody cheered.
UT1&2:	You're feeling sorry for yourself don't feel so sorry for yourself. You're feeling sorry for yourself, stop feeling sorry for yourself.

So have a nice death!

(After song UT1 &2 sit with feet on table)

UT1: So, how about a cup of tea missus?

UT2: And some biscuits?

NELL: No thanks, I'm not feeling too well.

UT2: Suit yourself.

UT1: We won't keep you any longer then. It was
fun doing business with you. And
remember... *(Lifting coffin)*

UT2: When you see an Undertaker,

UT1: Which won't be very often,

UT2: Just treat him like a Doctor,

UT1: And he'll help you with your coffin!

NELL: Go away, will you?! *(Holding door open)*

UT1: Oh.. and if you're ever passing, just pop into
the crematorium for a wee smoke!

(*NELL slams front door behind them , crosses room, and opens kitchen door*)

NELL: In you come, all clear!

MAGGIE: They've gone then? (*Enters carrying another plate*)

NELL: Thank god, I hate the thought of a dead man lying about the place.

MAGGIE: It makes a difference from two live ones lying about the place.

NELL: Don't you think we should have went to the funeral?

MAGGIE: No, he was only a guest.

NELL: It seems a shame Donald getting buried all alone.

MAGGIE: Go and jump in the hole with him if you feel like that.

NELL: No thanks, I'm going back up to sleep off this hangover. If Billy comes back tell him to keep quiet or I'll kill him.

UT1&2: (*Off*) 151!

MAGGIE: On you go Nell, don't worry about this, if the rats aren't hungry it'll do Billy tomorrow.

(*NELL exits, MAGGIE clears up a few things and goes into the kitchen. After a short pause there is a scream from NELL. MAGGIE returns*)

MAGGIE: Nell, was that you? (*NELL runs in*) Are you all right?

NELL: He's back!

MAGGIE: Who's back? What are you talking about?

NELL: Donald! In his bed!

MAGGIE: Who's in his bed?

NELL: He is, Donald!

MAGGIE: Oh, did he come back to get changed for the big occasion?

NELL: No, honestly, he's up there, I saw him!

MAGGIE: That's impossible, he was in his coffin
two minutes ago.

NELL: Go and look for yourself then, if you don't
believe me. He's definitely up there, as
large as life but.... smaller...

MAGGIE: Okay, you calm down, I'll go and see.

(*MAGGIE exits*)

NELL: Somebody must've moved him during the
night... unless.... Maggie!

(*MAGGIE returns*)

MAGGIE: You're right.

NELL: I told you...

MAGGIE: How the hell did he get back up there?

NELL: Maybe he wasn't dead at all. I've heard
about this before, he could have been in a
coma or just having a very deep sleep.

Maggie! Have you ever heard of the living dead?

MAGGIE: Who?

NELL: The living dead. Billy took me to see a film about them. "The Night of the Living Dead"

MAGGIE: And was Donald in it?

NELL: No, but there was a guy who looked like him in the sequel "The Night of the Twelve Dead"

MAGGIE: That's why they were putting the lid on before they went out. So that we couldn't see Donald when he wasn't there.

NELL: That's right!

MAGGIE: I knew Willie was up to no good. I can tell by the way he walks out of the door backwards.

(*There is a quick chap at the front door and Mr GRAY lets himself in*)

GRAY: Anybody home? Oh, good afternoon,

Simon Gray's the name, where's the bloke in charge? I caught this little advertisement in the paper. (*Indicating newspaper*) And I said to myself, "Why not pop around and have a little rummage?"

NELL: There's none left, the brewery....

MAGGIE: (*Grabbing newspaper*) Excuse me one moment sir. Nell, would you be kind enough to go upstairs and finish putting things away in Mr Macphersons room.

NELL: Away where? I'm not touching that...

MAGGIE: Just make it more.. presentable. I'll come and help you when I've finished with Mr Gray, thank you. (*Guides NELL upstairs*) Sorry about that, I'm Margaret Hare, my husband and I run the hotel.

GRAY: Actually, it's not the hotel I'm after, it's the property.

MAGGIE: We are of course selling as a going concern.

GRAY: How many guests do you have at the moment?

MAGGIE: At the moment.. er... two, no three!

GRAY: Rooms?

MAGGIE : Twelve.

GRAY: Staff?

MAGGIE: Only Willie and me.

GRAY: So, who was that?

MAGGIE: That was Nell, Mrs Burke, one of our guests.

GRAY: If you make your guests tidy other guests rooms, no wonder you only have three. Will Mr Macpherson be tidying Mrs Burke's room?

MAGGIE: No, Mr Macpherson was meant to be.. er... leaving us this morning but he seems to have changed his mind. Some people can't drag themselves away from our hospitality. Nell was only helping because we were busy.

GRAY: Busy? Three guests, nine empty beds? It's
hardly the New York Hilton. It doesn't
sound like much of a business venture.

MAGGIE: That's what we're selling it as, you can
dump toxic nuclear chemical waste in it if
you like. I don't care what you do with it.

GRAY: Then I'll book in shall I? I might as well
stay here and get to know the place. I can't
make a definite offer for a month though,
when Susan gets here, she's still in London,
I was just sent up to test the water.

MAGGIE: Double room for four weeks then, or
five?

GRAY: Single for four weeks, double for the fifth.

MAGGIE: We could get busy at this time of year.

GRAY: Avoiding unnecessary extravagance is the
reason that I have the ability to buy, and not,
probably, the reason that you have to sell.

MAGGIE: You're right. I wish you would explain
that to my husband.

GRAY: He's not one of these lazy, idle loafers that
     we keep reading about?

MAGGIE: No, he just has a surrealist interpretation
     of the word work, he thinks it means lie
     about all day and see how many different
     smells he can make.

GRAY: Pathetic isn't it? He'll never make any
     money like that.

MAGGIE: Maybe, but he wouldn't be too tight-
     arsed to spend it if he did.

GRAY: Nor would I, I'll take the double.

MAGGIE: Five weeks, one week in advance.
     *(GRAY pays her, MAGGIE gives him the
     key)* Number seven.

GRAY: I'll be back this evening then. If I don't
     decide to buy some other property this
     afternoon that is. Ha ha ha.. *(About to exit)*

MAGGIE: Oh, Mr Gray, could you do me a small
     favour by not saying anything about this to
     the other guests?. We don't want them
     leaving too early, do we?

GRAY: That's more like it. Looking after number one. (*Exits*)

MAGGIE: But talking a lot of number two. (*NELL enters*) Did you cover Donald?

NELL: Er... yes, I... covered him...

MAGGIE: What with?

NELL: The lining of my stomach.

MAGGIE: Oh, that would have helped if Mr Gray wanted a look round. "This is our last guest, as you can see, we have embalmed him, made him late for his own funeral, and laid him out with a fresh dry boak topping." Good old Scottish hospitality! Wait 'till I get a hold of that husband of mine, I'll kick his arse.

NELL: So will I!

MAGGIE: Don't bother, you can kick your own.

NELL: I wish I could and I'd join the circus.

MAGGIE: They'd better come home and get Donald out of that bed before Gray appears, or we'll all be in it.

NELL: What, Donald's bed?

MAGGIE: This place could really have been something special if they hadn't interfered. They're always jumping in at the deep end.

NELL: And Billy can't even swim.

(Sound of laughter outside, front door opens and BURKE and HARE enter with a large carry out.)

BURKE:..... and I said "That's not a monkey, that's his wife! " Ha ha ha!

(BURKE and HARE fall about laughing, they stop and look at MAGGIE, BURKE points at her and they start again.)

MAGGIE: Is that what you got at the Job Centre?

BURKE: Job Centre? I wouldn't be seen drunk in the place!

HARE: You won't find our style of work in a Job Centre.

MAGGIE: One question. Did either of you two smug bastards move Donald Macphersons body back into his room?

HARE: We were just going to tell you about that.

MAGGIE: So, you did.

HARE: He did.

BURKE: I did.

NELL: But why?

HARE: Because if we had left him here, they would have buried him.

BURKE: And he still owed you rent.

HARE: So, we took him from his coffin.

BURKE: And put him upstairs.

HARE: In his old room.

BURKE: And now we're going to bring him back down again.

HARE: Are we?

BURKE: Yes.

HARE: And now we're going to bring him back d......

MAGGIE: *(Interrupting.)* You're not moving any body, anywhere in my hotel until I know exactly what's happening.

HARE: Well...

NELL: Go right back to the bit about the Job Centre.

HARE: It's like this...

MAGGIE: You be quiet. Billy, you seem to be the.... ringleader, you explain.

BURKE: Right, when we woke up this morning we didn't have one single penny to rub together between us. And by our friends demise, you had lost a fair amount of the old royal bum paper.

MAGGIE: So?

BURKE: So, Willie and I put our heads together
and came up with a little scheme that'll
keep us in whisky for a good few weeks to
come.

MAGGIE: And are we going to hear the details of
this wonderful little scheme?

BURKE: Well, it's difficult to put into words
without sounding vulgar....

HARE: We flogged Donalds body.

MAGGIE: For a carry out?!

NELL: That's terrible!

MAGGIE: You could've got more than that!

BURKE: This was only a wee advance, until we
deliver, then we get the rest of the two
hundred pounds. *(Gives HARE a high five)*

MAGGIE: But, what if I'd taken Mr Gray up to see

the rooms?

HARE: Who's Mr Gray?

NELL: He's English.

BURKE: Oh him! Well that's narrowed it down to about forty five million.

MAGGIE: Mr Gray is our new guest, and he'll be back before tonight, so you'd better move that thing before we all end up in the clink.

BURKE: Don't worry, the only clinking you'll hear, is the clink of gold.

MAGGIE: What if they decide to look inside the coffin?

BURKE: It's just another job for them. they have as much respect for their customers as you have for yours, they'll throw it in a hole and forget it existed within five minutes.

MAGGIE: As long as you get it out of my house.

HARE: Right away Maggie.

MAGGIE: You can stick him with the bins. Mr Gray might want a look round the rooms.

NELL: Not the bin shed, it's not very nice, I liked Donald, not the bin shed.

MAGGIE: We'll have to put him somewhere that Gray won't find him. It's either that or your room.

NELL: Stick him with the bins.

BURKE: And we'll deliver him when it's dark, come back with the dosh, four bottles of Buckfast, four bottles of Thunderbird, four bottles of Eldorado and we'll have a well earned party!

(*NELL runs out about to be sick*)

HARE: Better make that just the three bottles of Buckfast.

SCENE 2

(A public park at night. There is a bench set at one side. HARE enters followed by BURKE who is counting a wad of £10 notes.)

HARE: Is there any more yet?

BURKE: One hundred and eighty quid, exactly!

HARE: Well, stop counting it, you're making me nervous, somebody might see us.

BURKE: And why not? Isn't a businessman allowed to count his takings in broad daylight?

HARE: It's dark.

BURKE: Broad moonlight then. *(Shouts)* Bring out your dead!

HARE: Shut up!

BURKE: What's wrong with you? I'm just trying to stir up some business.

HARE: Well, stir quietly. And stop fucking about

with that, give us my share.

BURKE: A share for Mr Hare. There you go....
fifty, sixty, seventy, ninety.

HARE: Hey! What happened to Eighty?

BURKE: Oh! Here it is. They must've been in the
wrong order.

HARE: Thank you very much!

BURKE: That was a piece of luck, Donald dying,
wasn't it?

HARE: Not for Donald!

BURKE: A very predictable answer, we can't
afford morals Willie, they're for the
satisfied working millions, not us. We've got
to grab these opportunities whenever they
come our way, or starve. We can't expect
this to happen every day.

HARE: We could.

BURKE: We could what?

HARE: Well, not every day, but we could still make a few bob now and then the same way.

BURKE: If you're talking about waiting until Mr Gray dies of a heart attack, you'll have a longer wait than Terry Waite.

HARE: I don't mean Gray.

BURKE: Actually it's a shame that we can't get hold of a couple like that, Knox admitted he'd pay through the nose for them.

HARE: Aye, and with a nose like that, we're talking big snotters.

BURKE: Pipedreams Willie, pipedreams.

HARE: What we need to do is attract more customers like Donald.

BURKE: Dead, you mean?

HARE: No, nearly dead.

BURKE: Oh aye. Of course you can have a room sir, as long as you promise to die within the next fortnight.

HARE: It's only an idea.

BURKE: You've enough trouble attracting guests without putting restrictions like that on them.

HARE: But we could invite certain people to stay in the hotel, offer them cheap digs. Auld jakies, druggies, hookers, steamers, bums, beasts, parasites, you know.

BURKE: Aye, but the Conservative party holds its conference in Brighton.

HARE: Or we could empty a couple of graves.

BURKE: Dr. Knox said he'd prefer them as fresh as possible, a few days under the ground and they'd be humming.

HARE: As long as it's not a tune.

BURKE: No, grave-robbing's not for us.

HARE: Where else can we get corpses then? Apart from actually doing away with somebody.

BURKE: Why not? I'm game for it. Why wait on the hand of fate when we can speed up the process?

HARE: Everybody's got to die sometime, right enough but it's a bit cheeky us deciding when.

BURKE: Not really, think of it as a more efficient form of euthanasia, recycling if you like.

HARE: But how do we recycle?

BURKE: Simple. Suffocation, no marks on the body.

HARE: We can't just walk up to people in the street and start suffocating them, we'd gather a crowd.

BURKE: Not if we take them home with us and get them that blootered that they crash out, and then... bye, bye wallop! Kiss the cushion cheerio.

HARE: And what about the actual....

BURKE: What about it?

HARE: Who does it?

BURKE: We both do. Toss a coin for the first and
then alternately, that means one each, just
me and you. I'm sure the girls won't mind if
we do all the dirty work.

HARE: God, I was forgetting about that. They
won't be too pleased.

BURKE: What, if they don't get a shot?

HARE: No, doing it in the first place.

BURKE: Nell and Maggie can have an equal share
of the profits and they don't even need to
lift a finger, or be anywhere near when we
do it. But we're the bosses, we're the
partners okay? And if we're careful, no one
will even suspect what we're up to. These
big bad wolves are going nowhere near the
little pigs house.

HARE: No chance!

BURKE: Partners?

HARE: Partners.

BURKE: Burke and Hare, put it there!

HARE: Hare and Burke, put it... er... Burke and Hare!

Music-MR BURKE AND MR HARE

Chorus1

BURKE:	I'm Mr Burke,
HARE:	I'm Mr Hare,
BURKE:	I'm over here,
HARE:	He's over there.
BOTH:	And when we meet you have a perfect pair.
	For everything we see we want we snare.
BURKE:	We've done it once,
HARE:	So why not twice,
BURKE:	The extra cash,
HARE:	Would be quite nice.
BOTH:	So lend an ear, we'll give you some advice,
	Don't you worry about the morals just the price.

Verse 1

HARE:	When I was down and out of luck, I didn't have a penny,
BURKE:	I came and split my cash in half although I hadn't any.
	When I was hungry, out of bread, I didn't have a farthing,
HARE:	Fifty-fifty's what I said and then we both were starving.

Chorus 2

BURKE:	I'm Mr Burke,
HARE:	I'm Mr Hare,
BURKE:	When I sit down,
HARE:	I'll be your chair.
BOTH:	Whenever you need me I'll be right there,
	And every day your burden I will bear.

BURKE:	If we stick in,
HARE:	For say a year,
BURKE:	Our future's bright,
HARE:	A good career.
BOTH:	Lots of cash for whisky wine and beer.
	It looks like our prosperity is clear.

Verse 2

HARE:	And if it came to court, then I'd be patiently remanded.
BURKE:	I'd admit the lot and say I did it single handed,
	If I were caught and you were not, I wouldn't do the singing.
HARE:	But I would take the blame myself and I would do your swinging.

Chorus 3

BURKE:	I'm Mr Burke,
HARE:	I'm Mr Hare,
BURKE:	I'm over here,
HARE:	He's over there.
BOTH:	We're strolling down your street so best beware,
	In case your body disappears into thin air,
	In case your body disappears into thin air.

BURKE: Right, come on. (*About to walk off*)

HARE: Hold on a second, toss the coin.

BURKE: Now?

HARE: Yes, now.

BURKE: Can't it wait?

HARE: No, if I don't know, I won't be able to get to sleep. I've got to prepare for things like this.

BURKE: Oh, you'll get to sleep all right. We're having a little celebration, remember?

HARE: Heads.

BURKE: Right now?

HARE: Go for it.

BURKE: Heads, you do the first?

HARE: No, heads you do the first.

BURKE: Give us a coin then ...

HARE: *(Pretends he has forgotten his prop.)* Er... I forgot to put it in my pocket...

BURKE: Well, I've not got one! What'll we do?

(They look at each other, then the audience, then each other. They jump into the audience, collecting loose change from various member's pockets, and return to the stage.)

BURKE: *(Tosses coin and catches it)* Shit.

HARE: Is it heads?

BURKE: No, tails, you won Willie.

HARE: Best of three!

BURKE: *(Tosses again)* Tails again.

HARE: Best of five!

BURKE: Again! It must be your lucky day. I'll just have to wait, I was quite looking forward to it as well.

HARE: If it means that much to you, I don't mind letting you go first...

BURKE: You're a good lad Willie, but you won fair and square. I'll get my turn soon enough.

HARE: But...

BURKE: Sssh, are you coming?

HARE: Er.. no, I think I'll hang about for a while to get me into the mood.

BURKE: You seem a bit nervous, second thoughts?

HARE: Who me? No danger!

BURKE: Right, I'll keep a glass warm for you. Happy hunting!

(BURKE exits. HARE paces up and down)

HARE: What chance have I got? It's either get a full time job or murder some poor bastard. I don't know if I can bring myself down to that level -working! But, if I do a nice easy one the pressure's on him. Finding an easy victim might be a problem though.

(ABIGAIL enters)

ABIGAIL: Excuse me son, could you help me out?

HARE: Fuck off, I've no change!

ABIGAIL: "I've no change", he says, "I've no change!" I'll have you know laddie, I'm not the begging type. I might not be rich but

I've got my pride.

HARE: Go and be proud at someone else then, I'm too busy.

ABIGAIL: Busy! If that's you busy I'd hate to see you standing around doing nothing.

HARE: Are you related to my wife?

ABIGAIL: I don't know what this world's coming to. You can't even ask a civil question without being abused. First person I meet in Edinburgh and you speak to me like that.

HARE: First person? *(Starts to take a good look at her)*

ABIGAIL: Aye, the bus got here half an hour ago, five minutes late by the way...

HARE: Terribly sorry then, welcome to Edinburgh.

ABIGAIL: That's more like it.

HARE: And where are you from?

ABIGAIL: Glasgow, my name's Abigail, Abigail

Simpson.

HARE: Pleased to meet you Abigail, William Hare.

ABIGAIL: Abbie.

HARE: Willie.

ABIGAIL: Willie Hare?... why not pube? Ha ha, that's what I'll call you!

HARE: Don't bother, I had enough of that at school.

ABIGAIL: There's no need to go into a huff.

HARE: I'm not in a huff, I'm used to it. What did you want anyway?

ABIGAIL: Actually I was looking for a bed for the night. I've been trying to find a cheap hotel, but everywhere seems to be full. You wouldn't know anywhere, would you?

HARE: *(Looks at her pensively but decides against it)* Er.. no. Have you tried down the Grassmarket? You might get something in one of the Hostels.

ABIGAIL: Aye, rabies! I'm not sleeping in the same place as all those old tramps, they gave me the shivers just thinking about them. I know what I'd do with them, I'd line them up, give them all a good wash, a decent set of clothes, a hot meal, and then I'd shoot the bastards! Bloody waste of public money!

HARE: That's a bit selfish.

ABIGAIL: Being selfish never hurt anyone.

HARE: Didn't it? That reminds me, I've got a hotel.

ABIGAIL: What?

HARE: I'll put you up for the night free of charge.

ABIGAIL: A hotel?

HARE: I know, I've got a memory like a council painter.

ABIGAIL: A hotel?

HARE: And there's a party starting right now.

You're more than welcome.

ABIGAIL: Are you sure?

HARE: Aye, come on, free booze, free food, free
        digs, what more could you ask for?

(HARE exits)

ABIGAIL: Oh well, he seems a nice enough young
        man... hold on curly I'm coming!

(She hurries after him)

SCENE 3

(Hare's Hotel the next morning, HARE is sitting at the table, BURKE enters from upstairs.)

BURKE: So?

HARE: I couldn't.

BURKE: You couldn't!

HARE: I was going to Billy, after the party, I went into her room last night but.... you know...

BURKE: It wasn't that last night when she kept calling you pube. Abigail was worth a lot more than Donald, even her handbag was worth a quick shuffle.

(BURKE produces a bundle of notes.)

HARE: Where did you?.... no you didn't, Billy, she'll get the Polis, she'll be getting up soon.

BURKE: It's not my fault she's getting up.

HARE: Okay, if you're so clever you go up and do it.

BURKE: I'd love to, but it's your turn Willie. Anyway, I'm away to cash my Giro and Mr Gray's promised to take me for a drink, since I'm skint. *(Puts Giro on the bar)*

HARE: But you're minted.

BURKE: Not as minted as he is. He's more minted than Mr Mint that owns all the big mint factories in Mintland.

HARE: Good, I'll come too.

BURKE: I think you should stay here. *(He throws Abigail's money in front of HARE.)* Either put that back, or we'll split it later.

(GRAY enters from upstairs)

GRAY: Ready Mr Burke?

BURKE: Just waiting on you Mr Gray.

GRAY: How about you? *(To HARE)* It's my shout.

BURKE: He's got a hangover.

HARE: No, I've not.

BURKE: Yes, you have!

HARE: Er.. no, thanks Mr Gray I'll stay here and see Abigail off.

GRAY: Oh yes, Abigail's leaving us this morning. That was a short stay.

BURKE: Yes, but it'll soon be over.

GRAY: Well, say goodbye for me. In case I don't see her again.

BURKE: Me too!

(BURKE and GRAY exit. HARE flicks through the banknotes, makes his mind up, lifts a cushion, try's it out on himself by holding it over his face and exits upstairs. Sound of footsteps, door opening, footsteps, silence then a loud scream. HARE enters again being chased by ABIGAIL in her nightdress.)

HARE: I was only bringing you an extra pillow.

ABIGAIL: You thieving pig, trying to take
　　advantage of me while I sleep. I'll show you
　　my young man. Come here...

(HARE keeps dodging behind furniture.)

HARE: I can explain, calm down, Abigail! For
　　gods sake, watch what you're doing. I'm
　　not a thief.

ABIGAIL: I caught you red handed, opening my
　　handbag and taking my money out, so don't
　　lie to me. I'll have the police on to you!
　　Standing over me counting it, of all the
　　cheek!

HARE: Er.. I was putting it back.

ABIGAIL: Putting it back! You shouldn't have
　　been taking it out in the first place!

*(Chase speeds up and ABIGAIL begins to throw
　　glasses etc.)*

ABIGAIL: Take that, and that...

*(ABIGAIL picks up a bottle and HARE ducks
　　behind the bar. ABIGAIL sinks slowly to the*

floor dying. HARE keeks over slowly to see
the cause of the silence. He notices
ABIGAIL and cautiously approaches her.)

HARE: Abigail, Abigail are you all right? I wasn't stealing your money... are you ill?... are you dead? *(He feels her pulse.)*

(BURKE enters)

BURKE: I won't get very far without a Giro to cash will I? *(Goes to pick up envelope, sees HARE'S face.)* Still building up the courage? What's up with your face? You look like you've just got a summons for a Restart interview. *(He sees body.)* You don't mess about do you?

HARE: I... I think it was a heart attack.

BURKE: *(Lifting cushion from floor near body.)* What we have here is a cardiac arrest, caused by an overdose of feathers being rammed doon the gub. Quick grab her legs, we'll put her in the alcove. *(They lift the body)*

HARE: It was an accident.

BURKE: Pull the other one!

HARE: I'm pulling them both!

(They put the body into the alcove and draw the curtain.)

BURKE: That should do for now. Willie, if it <u>was</u> a heart attack, you know what it means?

HARE: What?... oh no, no way, not me again!

BURKE: Well, save your alibi for the Judge. Two in two days, if we go on like this we'll be millionaires by Christmas.

HARE: I've not even shaved this morning and already I'm a thief and a murderer.

BURKE: There's no better way to start the day, gets your adrenaline going.

(MAGGIE and NELL enter from front door.)

MAGGIE: Morning boys. Mr Gray's waiting for you at the end of the street, Billy.

BURKE: He'll just have to wait then. We've got
      another customer. *(He opens the curtain.)*
      Tah nah!

NELL: Abigail! What happened?

BURKE: Willie?

HARE: Er.. I don't know.

MAGGIE: So, you decided to do it?

HARE: What?

BURKE: Have you been singing the song again?

HARE: I never said a word.

MAGGIE: You did actually, gibbering away in your
      sleep last night, the whole story, pacing up
      and down, talking to yourself, going in and
      out of her room. I was considering doing it
      for you to get a bit of peace and quiet.

BURKE: Talking in your sleep now?

NELL: You do it too.

BURKE: No, I don't.

NELL: Yes you do, you keep going on about sheep.

HARE: You dirty old farmer!

BURKE: Don't talk rubbish. I count them to help
me doze off.

HARE: Heard it.

BURKE: Anyway, I'd rather dream about sheep
than dead pensioners.

NELL: Yeuchh!

HARE: I didn't do it.

BURKE: You don't seem too bothered, Maggie.

MAGGIE: I don't care what you dream about, but
what are you going to do with her? Throw
her in the Forth, back into her room or sell
her like Donald.

NELL: Cellar? I didn't know we had a cellar.

BURKE: Or take no notice and earn yourself some

extra bananas.

MAGGIE: By bodysnatching?

NELL: What's bodysnatching?

MAGGIE: There was a lot of it in the nineteenth century, up-market grave-robbing for people who don't like getting their hands dirty.

BURKE: Who consider themselves above the toils of ordinary labour.

MAGGIE: Faint at the sight of sweat.

BURKE: Would rather expire than perspire.

HARE: Or in our case, just haven't got a shovel.

NELL: Our case?

BURKE: Willie and I that is. You reap the benefits, we'll reap the bodies!

NELL: Yeuchhh! I don't know about that!

BURKE: A good career move.

MAGGIE: Think of the money.

HARE: A world of pleasure.

BURKE: A life of leisure.

NELL: All right then, as long as it's not against the law.

Music-BODYSNATCHING BABY

Chorus 1
B&H: She's my bodysnatching baby, I'm her bodysnatching boy.
        When I see her snatch it drives me crazy, that's what I enjoy.
        She will be my favourite lady, I will be her only toy.
        She's my bodysnatching baby, I'm her
        bodysnatching boy.

Verse 1
MAGGIE: Maybe someday we could find some comfort in a bungalow
           a mortgage and a cruise around the world.
HARE: Make me happy tell me that you'll do it 'till the end
           for all the profit, for the Doctor for the will.

Chorus 1
N&M: I'm his bodysnatching baby, he's my bodysnatching boy,
        When he sees my snatch it drives him crazy,
        That's what he enjoys.
        I will be his perfect lady, he will be my only toy.
        I'm his bodysnatching baby, he's my bodysnatching boy.

Verse 2
NELL: I hope one day if we're still together we won't settle down,
           suburban town, let life become a bore.

BURKE: We'll be happy, life will be exciting, more exciting every day, I've tasted life and need some more.

Chorus 1 & 2 together

Ending
MAGGIE: Comfort,
NELL: Fun,
HARE: Money,
BURKE: On the run.
ALL: Is the quest of my success.
MAGGIE: Security,
NELL: Laughs,
HARE: Cash,
BURKE: Overdrafts.
ALL: Won't let me get depressed.
MAGGIE: Settle down,
NELL: Smile,
HARE: Take it easy,
BURKE: Run a mile.
ALL: Is the goal inside my mind.
MAGGIE: So we murder,
NELL: Catch,
HARE: Suffocate,
BURKE: Snatch.
ALL: For the benefit of mankind.
MAGGIE: So we murder,
NELL: Catch,
HARE: Suffocate,
BURKE: Snatch.
ALL: For the benefit of mankind.
MAGGIE: So we murder,
NELL: Catch,
HARE: Suffocate,
BURKE: Snatch.
ALL: For the benefit of mankind.

NELL: *(To Billy)* You can still be quite romantic at times, I didn't know you had it in you.

MAGGIE: Let's see what else you've got in you. It looks like the ball's in your court Billy.

NELL: Oh, Billy, your balls are in the court!

SCENE 4

(A street at night. After the interval and before the scene begins, a member of the audience begins to heckle. The cast peer round the curtain and try to quieten him, to no avail. BURKE and HARE then jump into the audience , beat him up, and carry him off. (He later becomes Jamie.) A drunk staggers on to the stage, followed by a POLICEMAN who takes him roughly by the arm and is about to lead him away. BURKE enters and pleads with the POLICEMAN to let the drunk go. The POLICEMAN gives him over, glad to be rid of him and exits. BURKE leads the drunk away. A prostitute leans at the side of the stage. HARE enters and sees her, he points her out to BURKE. BURKE sends him over. HARE whispers to her and she slaps his face. BURKE comes over and offers her money to leave with HARE. HARE leads her away. A man enters on crutches moving towards BURKE. BURKE strolls past, nodding hello and kicking the crutches away. He drags him away. The POLICEMAN enters again on the beat. HARE creeps up behind him with a baseball bat raised above his head. BURKE grabs

the bat just before HARE can hit him and runs off. The POLICEMAN turns around to find HARE standing with his hands in the air. HARE pretends he is trying to catch a butterfly and skips off. BURKE enters, HARE follows struggling with a large crate on a trolley. They are arguing.)

HARE: You looked as if you were enjoying it.

BURKE: Well, I didn't smell like it. It won't be that if you need a hand getting the next one.

HARE: Wait a minute. This was a fifty-fifty job. You needed my help. So, I reckon it's still you.

BURKE: All you did was hold him down.

HARE: And I carried him all the way up.

BURKE: And I carried yesterdays.

HARE: Yesterday's? There's a bit of a difference. You could have stuffed him in your pocket and jogged up.

BURKE: A body's a body, large or small, dead or

alive and I'll carry the next one as long as you admit it's your turn to do the despatch. *(He pulls out a Filofax.)* So far according to this....

HARE: What's that?

BURKE: A Filofax, Mr Gray gave it to me, helps me keep track of our business.

HARE: Have you written everything down?

BURKE: No, only names and prices, nothing suspicious.

HARE: Nothing suspicious?

BURKE: Very handy for times like this when we need information... now... so far, you've only done sixteen, ten of which I think Maggie may have had a hand in, and I've done seventeen, if you count Donald.

HARE: That wasn't you, he was pre-deed.

BURKE: It was my idea, anyway, Jamie here should count as about ten, if we ever get there. Have you got your breath back?

HARE: Aye, but hold on. I've been meaning to say to you... we've made a couple of quid now and we've hardly had time to spend it. Why don't we chuck it while we're ahead.

BURKE: Stop, you mean?

HARE: Just a break, a wee holiday, I'm getting fed up with dead bodies.

BURKE: Why? Are you turning vegetarian?

HARE: And we can't keep saying that people are away to Glasgow. Every time someone asks us, it's "Oh, he's away to Glasgow" or "She had to go to Glasgow". I know Glasgow's a dangerous place, but some people occasionally do come back alive.

BURKE: You're right Willie. It is getting too dangerous. We'll have to chuck it. *(Pause)* Better start saying they're away to Dundee.

HARE: Good idea!

BURKE: Come on.

(They are about to move the crate when GRAY enters.)

GRAY: Lovely evening for a walk gentlemen.

BURKE: Lovely Mr Gray.

HARE: Aye, smashin'.

GRAY: I'm heading home, if you're going that way. It's getting a bit late.

HARE: It always does at this time of night.

BURKE: I know, it's time we were going. Good night!

GRAY: And where are you two off to at this time of night?

BURKE: We could ask you the same question.

HARE: Yes, where are you two off to at this time of night?

GRAY: That's no secret, I was waiting at the station for the wife. She never appeared of course, probably decided to come tomorrow instead. I wasted all night sitting in that freezing cold station.

HARE: It's an M.G.C. you need. Marriage Guidance Counsellor.

BURKE: Or an S.M.G., Sub-Machine Gun. Ha ha! Good night Mr Gray!

GRAY: What's in the box?

BURKE: What box?

HARE: What box?

GRAY: That box.

BURKE: What box? I can't see any box.

GRAY: This box!

BURKE: Oh that box! It's a crate.

HARE: There's a crate in the box.

GRAY: And what's in the crate that's in the box?

HARE: Another smaller box?

BURKE: It's an antique!

HARE: That's right. We're going to a roadshow.

GRAY: What kind?

HARE: An antiques roadshow.

GRAY: No, what kind of antique?

HARE: An old one.

BURKE: And we've got to hurry before it gets any older. Good night.

(They are about to leave)

GRAY: I don't believe you! Antiques roadshows are held on Sunday afternoons, not Fridays at midnight.

BURKE: Aye, you're a clever man Mr Gray. There's not much that gets past you, is there?

GRAY: Now, go on, what is it?

BURKE: Promise not to tell anyone?

GRAY: Cross my heart and hope to die.

(BURKE gives HARE a smile)

BURKE: Very well... satellite dishes! We're just making a late delivery, if you know what I mean.

GRAY: Ah! The black economy eh?

BURKE: Right on the beak!

GRAY: So, that's where the extra cash has been coming from. Brilliant! There's nothing I appreciate more than a bit of free enterprise. The aphorism of Thatchers children! *(He spreads his arms out indicating the slogan.)*

HARE: What's aphorism?

BURKE: I don't know but it looks like rheumatism.

Music-MR GRAYS HAPPY DAYS

*I*ntro *(Spoken)*

GRAY: If we didn't have the criminals, the beggars or the poor,
          The alcoholic spongers, then the country would be pure.

	We could privatise the prisons
	and the army and the Queen,
	put the Great back in Great Britain
	and destroy this whole Shebeen.
	That's what I say!
B&H:	That's what he says!

(Rule Britannia)

Chorus

B&H:	What's that you say Mr Gray?
GRAY:	Things will be okay today, if everybody smiles they will be happy.
B&H:	Mr Gray what's that you say?
GRAY:	I can live the British way. I'm your average rich successful chappie.

Verse 1

GRAY:	You try to tell me that there's unemployment.
B&H:	Unemployment.
GRAY:	It's not my fault I didn't sack them all.
B&H:	He didn't sack us all.
GRAY:	I never let it spoil my own enjoyment.
B&H:	His enjoyment.
GRAY:	I simply slide my card into the wall.
B&H:	And grab some money,
GRAY:	Lots and lots of lovely money
B&H:	And grab some money,
GRAY:	Lots and lots of lovely cash.
ALL:	Hey!
B&H:	What's that you say Mr Gray?
GRAY:	Things will be okay today, if everybody smiles they will be happy.

(Rule Britannia)

Chorus

B&H:	What's that you say Mr Gray?
GRAY:	Things will be okay today, if everybody smiles they will be happy.

B&H:	Mr Gray what's that you say?
GRAY:	I can live the British way. I'm your average rich successful chappie.

Verse 2

GRAY:	Now don't you tell me you can't make a million.
B&H:	Make a million.
GRAY:	If I can do it anybody can.
HARE:	Who me?
BURKE:	Yes you.
HARE:	Oh good!
GRAY:	And with a bit of luck you'll make a killing.
B&H:	We'll make a killing.
GRAY:	And be the peoples favourite, worlds richest man.
B&H:	And grab some money,
GRAY:	Lots and lots of lovely money
B&H:	And grab some money,
GRAY:	Lots and lots of lovely cash.
ALL:	Hey!
B&H:	What's that you say Mr Gray?
GRAY:	Things will be okay today, if everybody smiles they will be happy.

Chorus

B&H:	What's that you say Mr Gray?
GRAY:	Things will be okay today, if everybody smiles they will be happy.
B&H:	Mr Gray what's that you say?
GRAY:	I can live the British way. I'm your average rich successful chappie.

Verse 3

GRAY:	Now don't you tell me of the worlds problems.
B&H:	Problems problems.
GRAY:	The starving millions or the ozone layer.
B&H:	Oh, forget them.
GRAY:	I don't need solutions I'm above them.
B&H:	Far above them.
GRAY:	For future generations I don't care.
ALL:	Because we won't be there.

Chorus

B&H: What's that you say Mr Gray?
GRAY: Things will be okay today, if everybody smiles
they will be happy.
B&H: Mr Gray what's that you say?
GRAY: I can live the British way. I'm your average
rich successful chappie.

GRAY: Tell you what, you'd better keep an eye out for the coppers. That box looks a bit shady.

BURKE: It's just the varnish.

HARE: You should try lifting it, it weighs a ton.

GRAY: Oh, put your back into it. Look, you're holding it at the wrong angle. Here, I'll show you... *(He takes hold of the trolley.)* God, you're right it is heavy... no, look it's not so bad once you get it balanced. *(He starts to move it around.)* There that's much better isn't it?

(The POLICEMAN enters, GRAY doesn't see him, BURKE and HARE run off.) No bother. Here steady it, will you? *(The POLICEMAN steadies the crate and helps GRAY stand it up.)* Now, you'd better move it before the pig... *(Double take on POLICEMAN. GRAY*

tries to walk away.) ...before the pig.. pig.. er... before the pig issue seller comes!

POLICEMAN : You can't leave that lying here all night, blocking the Queen's highway. Her Majesty could bump into it and get a skelf!

GRAY: It's err.... not really mine...

POLICEMAN : Then what are you doing with it on a trolley in the middle of the night?

GRAY: I was only testing the weight.

POLICEMAN : Not moving it somewhere without the owners prior consent, were we?

GRAY: No.

POLICEMAN : Just testing the weight? Do you do a lot of this weight testing then? Qualified weight tester are we?

GRAY: No, I found it here. I don't know who's it is.

POLICEMAN : And I suppose you haven't got a clue what's inside it? It was just lying here unattended.

GRAY: Well, yes.

POLICEMAN : In that case you won't mind
          coming back to the station to help us write
          your statement. Then we'll find out what it
          is and who it belongs to.

GRAY: Hold on... I... I might know who's it is.

POLICEMAN : Aha! Your memory coming back
          now is it. Just you get a hold of that trolley
          and come with me. Save your story for the
          Sergeant.

*(GRAY takes hold of the trolley under the watchful
          eye of the POLICEMAN. BURKE sneaks up
          behind POLICEMAN and knocks him to the
          ground with a Baseball bat, HARE takes
          the trolley from GRAY and exits.)*

GRAY: There was no need for that. He was only
          doing his job!

BURKE: So was Hitler.

GRAY: Is he dead?

BURKE: Aye, suicide, 1945.

GRAY: No, him!

BURKE: Don't be daft, you can't kill a policeman by hitting him on the head, there's nothing inside to damage. See you later. *(He exits)*

(GRAY has a look around and runs off. An old tramp enters, singing and moves towards the POLICEMAN. The POLICEMAN gradually rises and sees the tramp staring at him.)

POLICEMAN : Right! You'll do! Breach of the peace and police assault.

(He huckles the tramp off.)

SCENE 5

(Dr KNOX'S dissecting rooms, BURKE and HARE
have just placed JAMIE'S body on the
slab.)

KNOX: That'll do fine there lads. My, my, my, a
perfect specimen. Look at the size of him, if
he's as well built on the inside as he is on
the outside, my patients will be over the
moon. Excellent. It's a relief to see that
you're beginning to take some interest in
your work. A drink, gentlemen?

BURKE: Should we?

HARE: Why not?

BURKE: Certainly. What do you have Dr. Knox?

KNOX: There isn't exactly a name for it as yet,
I've been trying to perfect it for a couple of
months and I think it's nearly there. A cross
between surgical spirit and home brewed
whisky, with a few secret ingredients.

(He pours them a glass each.)

BURKE: Er.. thank you.

KNOX: You have the pleasure of being the first to try it, apart from myself of course, I live on the stuff, cheers!

(KNOX drinks his glass in one gulp.)

HARE: It smells like paint.

KNOX: It'll certainly put some colour in your cheeks.

HARE: Down the tonsils! *(Drinks it in one)* Jesus Christ! *(He staggers, falls on chair and bangs his head on the table a few times.)* Aaagh! That's brilliant! Try it Billy.

KNOX: Knox's elixir of life.

BURKE: Knox's tonic wine.

HARE: Knox your head off! *(Pouring another)*

KNOX: Help yourself Mr Hare, although I wouldn't advise more than three glasses on the first prescription. No more for me thanks, there's important work to be done before morning, and we don't want to start sending the wrong parts halfway round the world, it would upset the customers. It's not as if it's mail order Marital aids or something and they could send them back if they didn't fit correctly. *(Phone rings)* That might be another one now, excuse me. *(He lifts receiver)* Doctor Knox? Oh! hello Chris, how are you? Good. How's the wife? Goo-ood Excellent chance to practice your new skin grafting technique. Ha ha ha! But the Rolls is written off? That's a shame. What? Kidney transplant? You could be in luck, I've just had a delivery. I'll do some blood tests and get a flight time... oh! Private charter? Amazing what a little tax deductible index linked private medical insurance can do nowadays. Anything else? Eyes? Hundreds of them, I'll send you a box over to see you through the week. Cheerio then, bye! *(Replaces receiver)* A busy night ahead I think.

HARE: Here, Doctor, who was that?

BURKE: Shut up Willie! Don't ask Questions.

KNOX: Let him, no harm in telling you about the

unimaginable good that you two have been doing for medicine, and it's future, indeed the whole of mankind's future.

HARE: Us?

KNOX: Yes, you may not realise it, but you two probably do more good for mankind in one night than most people do in a lifetime.

HARE: Wait 'till I tell Maggie that!

KNOX: For instance. Did you know that since 1987, one heart has been transplanted every five minutes, day and night?

BURKE: Every five minutes, it must be getting frayed at the edges.

KNOX: I'm proud of you boys, you're doing a grand job.

BURKE : Nothing compared to your work Doctor.

KNOX: My work is easy, getting the subjects is the hard bit. Wherever you find them.

HARE: You mean, you don't know?

KNOX: Let's just say that I have a rough idea, and leave it at that. My conscience is cleared by the justness of the sacrifice.

HARE: *(To BURKE)* What does that mean?

BURKE: He's got an alibi for St Peter.

KNOX: An alibi for St. Peter? Perhaps, but first the B M A.!

Music-TRANSPLANT SURGERY

Intro
KNOX: If you've got to crack an egg to make an omelette,
Or kill a man to give a dog a bone,
And the world is better for it let society ignore it.
If it's somebody or something they don't own.
We justify sadistic pleasure daily,
We organise our critics with a sneer,
Without regret we will enjoy it. If it's living
we'll destroy it
for the quality of life we love so dear.

ALL: One more life won't make a speck of difference,

as a sacrifice to save a hundred more.
And a hundred more than evens up the score.

Build
BURKE: Transplant surgery!
HARE: Transplant surgery!
KNOX: Transplant surgery's
ALL: What it's all about!

Verse 1

KNOX: Transplant surgery's what it's all about.
We're pruning the population in medicines final bout.
If you want to put the kidneys in, you've got to take them out.
Transplant surgery's what it's all about.
Transplant surgery's what it's all about.
The future of the Human race has always been in doubt.
When I perfect immortal life, the people they will shout,
Transplant surgery's what it's all about.

Middle

Hearts, lungs, liver and Kidneys, hair upon your head.
Skin graft emergency to stop you being dead.
Frontal lobotomy, spare parts are brought to me,
I'll even swap your eyes.
I get a taste of waste when anybody dies.

Verse 2

Transplant surgery, I hope that you agree,
Is good for health, increases wealth and life expectancy.
If you supply the honey I'll be busy as a bee,
Transplant surgery, I hope that you agree.
Transplant surgery, I hope that you agree,
Decomposing corpses are becoming history.
They used to go to Heaven, but now they come to me.
Transplant surgery, I hope that you agree.

Build

BURKE: Transplant surgery!
HARE: Transplant surgery!
KNOX: Transplant surgery!
ALL: We hope that you agree!

BURKE: Obviously we don't want to hold you
back from your heavy schedule Doctor. So,
if you could just square us up, before Willie

96

settles down for the night, we'll be off.

KNOX: As you wish Mr Burke. Now, where's my chequebook?

BURKE: Chequebook! If it's all the same Doctor we'd rather have cash as usual.

KNOX: I don't believe I have enough cash lying around. I was going to give you small bonus.

BURKE: Very kind of you Doctor.

KNOX: It'll encourage you to collect more specimens like this. The junk you've gathered over the past few months has been useless for anything but experiments, even the N.H.S. wouldn't touch it.

BURKE: Doctor, we bring you the best quality stuff we can get our hands on.

KNOX: The only quality most of your previous cadavers have had is alcoholic content. I was playing with the idea of fermenting some of their livers in my home brew.

HARE: *(Who is still drinking away, has glass at his lips and spits it out.)* What?

KNOX: Relax Mr Hare, I didn't. If you're that desperate for cash, we could wander along to the card in the wall machine.

BURKE: That'll do nicely. Are you coming Willie?

HARE: *(Trying to stand up)* Aye, hold on... *(Falls back on to seat)* On the other hand I'll just stay and look after the pub while you're gone.*(He falls asleep)*

(KNOX and BURKE exit laughing. HARE awakes.)
I'll get a round in while you're gone... where's the bar?... barman!... no waitress service? Typical... what kind of place is this?.. I'll find it... *(Stands up)* ... up you get Willie, that's a boy... now... barman!... barman!... where is he ?.. no wonder I couldn't find it, looks more like a hospital to me, these interior designers want shot. Barman!.. *(Sees JAMIE)* Oh there you are. What are lying there for? Having a wee nap? Right enough it's dead tonight, you can afford to.. well... are you going to serve me?... wake up!... oh suit yourself.. I'll pour

it... put it on my slate, if you remember, cos I won't... I think somebody's been drinking on the job, haven't they?... whoops! Better sit down again Willie... *(Takes a half bottle of Knox's brew and slides it into his pocket)* A wee carry out for later on.... what time do you close at Barman?... I wonder where Billy's got to, he'd love this, self service, reasonable prices, unconscious bar-staff!... wait a minute... I've seen him before somewhere... where was it? ... oh it doesn't matter...

(HARE sits staring at the body. It slowly rises, sits up, stands and walks towards him.)

HARE: Sobered up then?

JAMIE: William Hare, liar, murderer, thief!

HARE: I was going to pay for the drink, but you wouldn't wake up.

JAMIE: I don't want your money!

HARE: Good, can I have another one then? *(JAMIE knocks the glass from his hand.)* I take it that's a no?

JAMIE: Murderer!

HARE: I've not murdered anyone. Not today
anyway.

JAMIE: What about me?

HARE: You're a murderer?

JAMIE: Twelve hours ago I was alive and well, and
walking the earth.

HARE: It's not my fault if you like a good bevy.
What's it got to do with me if you lie about
the bar steaming.

JAMIE: You killed me - remember?

HARE: Jamie?!

JAMIE: Yes!

HARE: But how... ?

JAMIE: I have returned to torment you for your
evil deeds and I will return again and again.

HARE: Again and again?

JAMIE: And again and again and again.

HARE: Oh no!

JAMIE: And again and again and again and...

HARE: All right I've got the message. But I didn't kill you Jamie, it was Burke!

JAMIE: It was you both. Equally you bear the guilt, and singly I, the pain, which you so crudely justify, and I will so explain ...

Music-TRANSPLANT SURGERY PART 2

Verse

JAMIE: Transplant surgery like water into wine,
I don't like being selfish but you've got to draw the line.
Of all the bodies in the world, why did you pick on mine?
Transplant surgery like water into wine.
Transplant surgery like water into wine,
I never had a donor card, I never chose to sign.
I should have been alive and well, but now I'm quite supine.
Transplant surgery like water into wine.

Middle

My Heart, lungs, liver and Kidneys, hair upon my head.
Skin graft emergency to stop you being dead.
(Now I'm dead instead.)
Frontal lobotomy, spare parts are brought from me.
You'll even take my eyes.

I got a taste of waste when my old body died.

Outro (as Knox's Intro)
So.. if you've got to crack this egg to make your omelette,
Or kill this man to give your dog a bone.
And your world is better for it, let society ignore it,
If I'm somebody or something you don't own.

(JAMIE returns to the slab. HARE takes a closer look.)

HARE: Oh, bugger this!

(He is about to run out of the door, when BURKE and KNOX return.)

HARE: That was a nightmare. He was walking about talking to me!

KNOX: Good stuff, isn't it?

HARE: Honest.

BURKE: Calm down Willie. Er.. Doctor, why don't you explain the latest requirements to Mr Hare?

KNOX: Very well, pay attention Mr Hare. Amongst my patients, I have a certain lady, an actress, retired of course, but she was once very, very beautiful. Now, after all of the good living that came along with the success, and with age eating away at her, she has lost her beauty somewhat. She lives like a recluse to avoid the glare of bad publicity. The stale stench of her savings grows daily in size and impotence, yet for some reason, she doesn't like the thought of sticking it in her will.

HARE: And I don't like the thought of sticking my will in her, scared to go out? She must have a face like a baboon with piles.

KNOX: A rather inelegant definition of her vanity. But, yes. And so I have been blessed with the opportunity to realise one of my lifelong ambitions: a complete surgical transformation! *(He removes a photograph from his pocket)* Here's an old photograph, vital statistics on the back. *(He gives it to BURKE)*

BURKE: She's got some vital statistics on her front.

KNOX: And as fresh as possible.

BURKE: As fresh as the morning dew!

HARE: Aye, as fresh as that old Jew, we got you the other morning.

(BURKE and HARE exit, KNOX sits at his desk with his back to JAMIE.)

KNOX: Now, where was I? Ah, here we are... *(Singing)* "I left my heart in San Francisco... "

(JAMIE rises again and walks towards KNOX, but KNOX turns around and shoots him just in time.)

KNOX: *(To audience)* You just can't get the staff nowadays.

SCENE 6

(Hares Hotel. BURKE and HARE enter from upstairs.)

BURKE: We'll have to get rid of that one, it's beginning to smell like Rutherglen. Trust you to snatch a Tory M.P.

HARE: How was I supposed to know? She was dressed as a tramp and sleeping in a cardboard box. It looked like an easy target so I just got tore in.

BURKE: Aye, but the box had 'Harrods' stamped on the side. You've got to watch out for things like that. These M.P.s enjoy sleeping rough every now and then, just to prove that a man can live on five pounds a week. It's a great vote winner in the south.

HARE: And what about Mr Gray, he's still haunting the place. They might come here looking for him... he would tell them about the satellite dishes!

BURKE: What satellite dishes?

HARE: In the crate.

BURKE: They don't exist.

HARE: That wouldn't put them off, they'd jail us anyway. They might want to search the house!

BURKE: Rubbish! If a policeman ever walked through that door... I'd drink a toast through one of your socks!

HARE: It's a deal.

(POLICEMAN enters.)

BURKE and HARE: Morning officer! *(Double take.)*

POLICEMAN: This is it. Hares Hotel. Good day gentlemen. Now, who's who?

(No-one answers.)

Well?

HARE: I'm er... Mr Hare... er... Willie Hare, pube. I

mean William Hare, officer...

POLICEMAN: That means you're the one I'm looking for! *(Indicating BURKE.)*

BURKE: Me?

POLICEMAN: I've been having a little chat with your wife, and she's told me all about you, you naughty boy.

BURKE: When?

POLICEMAN: Just now. We had a very interesting discussion on the way from the station. She's waiting in the car with my partner, outside.

HARE: Oh, Constable Outside, I know him!

POLICEMAN: Shut it!

BURKE: What has she been saying?

POLICEMAN: You're about to find out. I was just confirming that you were here.

(POLICEMAN exits.)

BURKE: I don't believe it, Nell wouldn't grass us, not intentionally.

HARE: Where did she go this morning?

BURKE: She was walking Maggie down to the Bingo. She must've started blethering to the Polis.

HARE: That's out of order! You can't trust anybody, I wanted to go to the Bingo!

BURKE: Quick hide her before the Polis come back. I'll keep them occupied.

(HARE exits upstairs. BURKE takes out his Filofax and hides it under a cushion. POLICEMAN enters carrying luggage, followed by the stunningly beautiful MRS GRAY.)

POLICEMAN: There we are, a happy couple re-united.

MRS GRAY: That's not my husband!

POLICEMAN: It's not?

MRS GRAY: No.

POLICEMAN: I'm sorry, I thought you were Mr Gray...

BURKE: Sadly, no. Mr William Burke, at your service, and yours darli.. er.. Mrs Gray?

MRS GRAY: Thank you Mr Burke, I take it we do have the right hotel?

POLICEMAN: Then where is Mr Gray?

MRS GRAY: Yes, where is Simon?

BURKE: Probably looking for you, he went to meet your train.

MRS GRAY: Well, I'll just wait here, if you don't mind. Thank you officer. *(She gives him a tip.)*

POLICEMAN: Thank you Ma'am. I'll tell you what I'll do, if you give me a description of your husband and I see him at the station, I'll run him back.

BURKE: Description!

MRS GRAY: Well, he's quite slim...

BURKE: No, no, he's fat, really fat.

MRS GRAY: What?

BURKE: He's been eating a lot since he arrived, you'd hardly recognise him, he's put on an unbelievable amount of weight in since last month. He's about 22 stone now!

MRS GRAY: My God!

POLICEMAN: *(Writing)* Slim, fat, yes..

MRS GRAY: Brown hair...

BURKE: No, green hair, he dyed it last week.

POLICEMAN: Green hair...

BURKE: And he's wearing a white boiler suit with pink Doc Marten boots and yellow star shaped glasses, and he's learning to play the guitar.

MRS GRAY: Guitar? I don't believe it!

BURKE: It's true.

POLICEMAN: Okay. Slim, fat, white boiler suit, pink Doc Marten boots, yellow star shaped glasses, brown and green hair and learning to play the guitar... sounds familiar. I'm sure we'll spot him soon.

BURKE: You can't miss him.

POLICEMAN: Meanwhile, I'll leave you in the safe hands of Mr Burke, crime doesn't stop for lunch as they say!

MRS GRAY: Cheerio, and thanks again. *(POLICEMAN exits)* It's amazing that he could have changed so much in four weeks. Has he become a new age hippy? Or a punk rocker? Or a morris dancer? Or, heaven forbid, a new age punk- hippy-morris-dancer?

BURKE: No.

MRS GRAY: No?

BURKE: No, because it's not exactly true.

MRS GRAY: About the green hair?

BURKE: About everything, he looks the same as he
always has.

MRS GRAY: Then why did you say...?

BURKE: Last night, that same officer, was knocked
unconscious as he was about to arrest your
husband. He hasn't got a clue about his
name, but he won't forget his face in a
hurry. That's why I gave a false description,
to protect Simon.

MRS GRAY: You could have been arrested
yourself, because of that idiot!

BURKE: Oh, don't mention it.

MRS GRAY: You know, there are days when I wish
I'd never met him.

BURKE: Don't say that, he's a good lad really.
Maybe he just doesn't know how to
appreciate a good woman like you.

MRS GRAY: You're a very kind man Mr Burke.

Has anyone ever told you that?

BURKE: Not for a while, no. And there's no need to be so formal, call me Billy.

MRS GRAY: Billy. If only I had met a man like you four years ago.

BURKE: Well, I'll be waiting here for you if you ever have second thoughts.

MRS GRAY: *(Giggling)* Mind what you say, Billy. I might be tempted to take you up on that offer one day.

BURKE: One day? How about today? *(He tries to kiss her.)*

MRS GRAY: Stop! *(Pulling away)* Behave yourself Mr Burke, I didn't mean that. I was only being friendly.

BURKE: Oh make your mind up.

MRS GRAY: What?

BURKE: You were leading me on like a bitch up a butchers close.

MRS GRAY: I most certainly was not!

Music-FIRST YOU WILL

Chorus 1
BURKE:
First you will and then you won't,
Say you love me, then you don't.
Just fall in love with me, baby can't you see?
Oh how happy we would be, if you fell in love with me.

Chorus 2
First you stop and then you start,
Break your promise, break my heart,
Just fall in love with me, baby can't you see?
Oh how happy we would be, if you fell in love with me.

Verse 1
Sometimes you tell me, that life is good,
And sometimes you never try as hard as you could.
Sometimes you're lazy, sometimes you're sad,
And sometimes you change your mind
and that just drives me mad.

Chorus 3
First you laugh and then you cry,
Tell me no and say goodbye,
Just fall in love with me, baby can't you see?
Oh how happy we would be, if you fell in love with me.

Verse 2
Every night I'll stand out side your house in soaking rain.
You'll tell me to come in and then you'll change your mind again.
I could wait for years you know, but baby can't you see?
We could start again right now if you would just agree.

Chorus 1
First you will and then you won't,

Say you love me, then you don't.
Just fall in love with me, baby can't you see?
Oh how happy we would be, if you fell in love with me.
Just fall in love with me, baby can't you see?
Oh how happy we would be, if you fell in love with me.

(BURKE sits down and pours himself a drink. MRS GRAY sits beside him.)

MRS GRAY: Don't I get one?

BURKE: I didn't think you wanted one. Do you?

MRS GRAY: No, but thanks for the offer. I'm sorry Billy but... no hard feelings?

BURKE: They're away now. Maybe some other time... eh?

MRS GRAY: That's better. *(She pecks him on the cheek)* I'll go upstairs and unpack now.

BURKE: If you like... no! You can't!

MRS GRAY: What do you mean, if you like, no, you can't?

(BURKE blocks her way to the upstairs door)

BURKE: You can't.

(NELL enters from front door)

NELL: Can't what?

BURKE: Go upstairs.

NELL: Why can't she go upstairs? Why do you want to go upstairs? Who is she?

BURKE: Nell, this is Mrs Gray, Mr Gray's wife. Mrs Gray, this is Nell, my er... wife. I'll take these, *(Grabbing suitcases)* There's no need for you to go up just yet.

NELL: What's got into you?

MRS GRAY: He's got very energetic all of a sudden.

NELL: That usually only happens at night, he'll be fast asleep in a few seconds.

MRS GRAY: If you'd like to show me the way please, Nell. I think I'll manage myself.

BURKE: Mrs Gray, you can't. The rooms need a

good dusting... Nell?

NELL: No they don't, the sheets just need changed... *(BURKE pokes her in the eye.)* Ow!

BURKE: Yes they do!

MRS GRAY: Are you trying to cover up for my husband again, let me see for myself.

(She moves towards the door.)

BURKE: Okay, okay, if you don't believe me. (He *takes the handle of the door and pretend to pull.)* Oh no, it's locked, and we don't have a key! So now nobody can go upstairs!

NELL: That's why the rooms are so dusty.

MRS GRAY: Let me try.

BURKE: It won't budge. (As *if struggling)* I've been trying all morning. I'm telling you, we won't open that door until we find the key or rip it from it's hinges, or may God strike me dead! *(He opens his arms wide, waiting for God to strike him dead. Nothing happens.)* See, I told you! (HARE *enters through the door)* Silly me! You're meant to push it, I've been pulling it all morning! Is everything clean Willie?

HARE: Aye, except the sound of your conversation.

BURKE: This is the proprietor, Mr Hare. Mrs Gray, your room awaits!

MRS GRAY: Then it can await a little longer. If I'm finally allowed to see inside I'm sure to find nothing of interest. I'll go back to the station and try to find Simon before the police do. And if he shows his face here, tell him to stay put. I'll see enough of the hotel before long, if we decide to buy it. Cases Mr Burke, thank you, just leave them in my room.

(BURKE lifts the cases, MRS GRAY exits, BURKE drops the cases and crosses to HARE. NELL takes cases and exits.)

BURKE: Decide to buy? The hotel? What's this?

HARE: It was Maggies idea, when we were skint. She was going to sell the business to the

Grays, but she's changed her mind.

BURKE: That's okay then. Did you get rid of our Conservative chum?

HARE: She's under some tarpaulin and sheets in the big airing cupboard.

BURKE: It makes a change, us canvassing one of them, doesn't it?

HARE: What was that Polis after?

BURKE: Not us, so don't panic. All we have to concern ourselves with is getting the Doctor his dinner.

HARE: Did you notice Mrs Gray?

BURKE: A fine looking woman, what about her?

HARE: Did she remind you of anyone?

BURKE: Now that you mention it, she does...

HARE: Look at the photo Knox gave us.

BURKE: *(Taking out photograph and kissing it)*

That's amazing it's her!

HARE: Problem solved.

BURKE :Her husband would be slightly annoyed at us.

HARE: Take both of them. One each.

BURKE: Oh? Listen to fucking Atilla! Take both of them? And the policeman too I suppose? No, they're well out of our league. The Grays are B.U.P.A. patients not to be confused with B.U.P.A. supplies.

HARE: What a waste, Knox would have paid an arm and a leg for them.

BURKE: Unfortunately, we don't do part exchange. Anyway, Mrs Gray fancies me you know.

HARE: You, you must be joking, ha ha ..

BURKE: Laugh if you will, but I can tell.

HARE: But Billy, we'll never get a closer match.

BURKE: That's why we're leaving now, it gives us

more time for a belligerent browse.

*(BURKE and HARE exit. NELL enters from
upstairs just as the front door is closing, she
opens the font door and calls after them.)*

NELL: Billy! Where are you going now? What?
Again? Well, get a loaf while you're out, I
forgot. *(She closes the door)* Aye, and if
he forgets, he'll forget that he forgot, but he
won't forget that I forgot ... is that right?
Oh, near enough. *(Finds BURKE'S Filofax)*
Oh! A Fileyfax! It must be Mr Gray's. *(Puts
it on the bar)* So, I'm stuck in here myself
again! Oh well, I could do with the peace
and quiet, there's always too much going on
in here. Billy better watch himself, if the
Social Security find out he's working, he'll
get his Giro stopped. *(GRAY enters, out of
breath)* Hiya!

GRAY: Has my wife arrived yet?

NELL: Aye, she's here, but she's not here.

GRAY: Pardon?

NELL: She was here to see if you were here, but

she's away because you weren't, even though you are.

GRAY: Pardon?

NELL: If you were here when she was here, she wouldn't have went away, then she would have been here when you got here.

GRAY: I don't understand! Where is she?

NELL: Are you daft? She's at the Train Station, and so are the police, so you've to stay here.

GRAY: Police?

NELL: Yes, they were looking for you too. I'll go and fix your room up before Mrs Gray comes back. Oh, your wee book's on the bar.

(NELL exits upstairs, GRAY goes over to the bar and picks up the Filofax)

GRAY: Wee book? Oh, it's the one I gave to Billy. *(Begins to read)* What's this? Donald MacPherson, I wonder what happened to him? ..Two hundred pounds, Abigail

Simpson, three hundred pounds. *(Flicks through the pages)* M.P. must be someone's initials ... cancelled! Jamie, five hundred pounds! Special order for Dr Knox, Mrs 'x'? Yesterday's date. Hmm, must be for the satellite dishes, a bit expensive though, it can't be that...

(NELL screams from upstairs. GRAY runs upstairs, dropping Filofax. After a short pause, GRAY screams. NELL enters, followed by GRAY)

GRAY: What's going on here? Where did that come from?

NELL: I got more of a fright than you. They don't usually keep them in that cupboard.

GRAY: I knew there was something weird going on in here! A dead body wrapped in sheets! Who was it?

NELL: It must've been Willie, he's always leaving them in stupid places, unhygienic if you ask me.

GRAY: Whose corpse was it? *(He sees the Filofax*

lying where he dropped it and picks it up slowly.) Wait a minute, that's it... Donald, Abigail, all of those bed and breakfast customers who never appeared at breakfast! Oh my God! I'm going for the police, I'm not staying here a second longer. *(He backs out of the door)* Help!!

NELL: *(Calling after him)* If it's the sheets you're worried about, I've got plenty more clean ones! Oh dear, Maggie's going to be upset if I have to disturb her at the Bingo.

(NELL exits)

SCENE 7

(Same location as Scene 2. BURKE and HARE are sitting on the bench.)

HARE: When have you ever seen a woman fitting Knox's description better than Mrs Gray? Never!

BURKE: Look, we don't need an exact replica.

HARE: I say we take her.

BURKE: And I say we don't.

HARE: We might as well chuck it then, because, A- we've got to find Mrs Gray's double, B- she's got to like the drink enough to come back with us, and C- if we do, you'll probably want to shag her too!

BURKE: It's already been discussed and I decided that we leave her alone. Another thing, I don't want to shag her, she wants to shag me. I've seen the twinkle in her eye.

HARE: And felt the twinkle in your winkle. Listen Billy, you're the one who said we should compromise at times like this, so why don't we... *(HARE whispers in BURKE'S ear. BURKE stands up angrily.)*

BURKE: You're sick Willie!

HARE: *(Standing)* I know, I'm sick of you getting your own way.

(GRAY enters looking over his shoulder and runs straight into the arms of HARE)

HARE: What's the big hurry? Still looking for your wife? It seems there's a few people after her today, a very popular lady.

(GRAY backs into BURKE)

BURKE: Mr Gray! What have you been up to? You're sweating like a paedophile in a creche!

GRAY: I was running, er, jogging, you've got to keep in shape, you know.

HARE: What did you do? A hundred laps of the castle? Here take some of this. Keep fit in a bottle. *(Offering him a bottle of Whisky)*

GRAY: Thanks, but I really must get going again...

HARE: Nonsense. *(Giving him bottle)* Tell you what, there's not much left, you finish it, it's like liquid valium. Billy, I'm going back to the hotel.

BURKE: What for?

HARE: I'd better tell Mrs Gray where her husband is.

BURKE: I'll walk you along if you don't mind, keep you out of trouble.

(BURKE and HARE exit. GRAY watches them go, bottle in hand)

GRAY: Bloody hell! What if she goes back and they're waiting on her? I couldn't handle two of them, I'd better get the filth. But what if it's too late? What will I do? I'll have a drink of this. *(Finishes bottle)* That's better, right, *(He turns and runs into the arms of the POLICEMAN)* Aaaah!

POLICEMAN: Watch where you're going sir. Ooh!

It's you! I knew I'd run into you sooner or later. You're jailed boyo! Attempted theft and assaulting a police officer. Time for a wee holiday. *(Putting cuffs on GRAY)*

GRAY: You've got the wrong man! Those two along the street, they're murderers!

POLICEMAN: Are they? Good for them!

GRAY: Yes, you should be arresting them not me. It's Burke and Hare you want.

POLICEMAN: I happen to have had the pleasure of meeting Mr Burke and Mr Hare, and they do not strike me as being murderers. Whereas you, I know personally are a crook, Mr... name please?

GRAY: Gray.

POLICEMAN: Address?

GRAY: Hares Hotel, Tanners Close.

POLICEMAN: Are you trying to take the piss? I have here an exact description of Mr Gray of Hares Hotel, Tanners Close, and he most definitely looks nothing like you.

GRAY: But my wife, I can't find her, her life might be in danger.

POLICEMAN: She'll be quite safe as soon as we get you behind bars. Now, come on, let's go and tell the sergeant a nice bedtime story. Move it!

GRAY: But, but...

(MR GRAY II walks past wearing a white boiler suit, pink Doc Martens, yellow glasses and trying to play the guitar)

POLICEMAN: See, do you think I'm stupid? That's Mr Gray!

(POLICEMAN escorts GRAY off)

SCENE 8

(Hares Hotel. Mrs Gray is sitting with her back to the door, unwrapping parcels. BURKE and HARE enter behind her.)

HARE: Ah, Mrs Gray, I see you're back.

MRS GRAY: You'd have to be bloody clever to see my front from there!

(BURKE and HARE have a silent argument behind her, BURKE sits beside her, HARE bolts the door.)

BURKE: And what have we been buying today then? A small present for the latest man in your life?

MRS GRAY: You never give up do you?

BURKE: Nope.

(HARE sits beside them and produces the bottle he stole from Knox's surgery.)

HARE: There's a wee drink for you, a welcome to Edinburgh. One of our pals makes this stuff. Cheers!

BURKE: Absent friends!

(BURKE and HARE laugh and empty their glasses but MRS GRAY doesn't touch it.)

MRS GRAY: Sorry, gentlemen, I don't believe in it. Alcohol very rarely passes my lips.

BURKE: Why? Are you one of these people that inject it? Go on...

MRS GRAY: No, thank you.

BURKE: A wee tiny sip won't do you any harm, taste it...

HARE: On you go...

(MRS GRAY takes a sip)

MRS GRAY: Mmm, quite strong isn't it?

BURKE: *(Patronisingly)* Aw, too strong for you? Do you want some lemonade instead?

MRS GRAY: I'm a big girl Mr Burke, I can look after myself.

(She empties her glass and starts to cough.)

BURKE: What did I tell you?

HARE: Have another one to clear your chest.

(He fills her glass and gives BURKE another glass with a sock over it. BURKE removes it.)

BURKE: Careful Willie, we don't want Mrs Gray lying on her back unconscious, do we?

HARE: *(Smiling)* No-o!

MRS GRAY: I can handle it.

(MRS GRAY finishes another glass)

BURKE: Cheers!

HARE: Cheers! It looks as if we might be busy tonight.

MRS GRAY: Oh, have the night off, we'll have a party, hic, hic, excuse me gentlemen, I think I'm going to... *(She stands up and staggers)* I don't feel at all well... *(She falls back into BURKE'S hands.)*

BURKE: You feel all right to me! *(He carries her over to the alcove and lies her down, gently.)* That's it darling, lie down and sleep it off.

(HARE lifts a cushion and throws it to BURKE.)

HARE: On you go! You're on the bell Billy, give her a good night kiss!

(BURKE goes back to her with the cushion and holds it above her head.)

BURKE: I'm sorry about this but... (He *lifts her head and places the cushion underneath.)* ...I won't destroy a work of art.

HARE: Okay, I will. Whether it's your turn or not. (Getting *another cushion*)

BURKE: Fancy your chances Willie? *(HARE stops)* What's keeping you?

HARE: I'm just calculating what kind of price the Doctor would pay for you.

Music-YOUR ATTITUDE IS CRAZY

Verse 1

HARE:	Your attitude is crazy.
BURKE:	Your memory is hazy.
HARE:	I trusted you.
BURKE:	I'm watching you.
HARE:	I'm right.

BURKE:	You're wrong.
HARE:	You're wrong
BURKE:	I'm right.

Verse 2

HARE:	I'm sick of you being lazy.
BURKE:	You'd better stop picking my daisy.
HARE:	I'm asking you.
BURKE:	I'm answering you.
HARE:	I'm right.
BURKE:	You're wrong.
HARE:	You're wrong.
BURKE:	I'm right.

Chorus 1

BOTH:	You, never really knew me,
BURKE:	Now that you do, what do you think?
HARE:	I think you stink.
BURKE:	And so do you.
BOTH:	You, never could see through me.
HARE:	Now that you do, what do you see?
BURKE:	I should've had a guarantee.

Middle 1

BURKE:	For you I've got an ultimatum, it's time we sorted out a thing or two.
HARE:	It's time we had some real verbatim. Our partnership is under review.
BURKE:	If I can't trust you I don't need you find some other fool to lead you, you've not got long you'd better start to pray.
HARE:	There's nothing more disgusting than a man who won't admit defeat and boy are you disgusting me today.

Verse 3

BURKE:	You're targeting my good friend.
HARE:	I think you mean your nude friend.
BURKE:	I'm warning you.
HARE:	Informing you.
HARE:	I'm right.
BURKE:	You're wrong.

HARE:	You're wrong.
BURKE:	I'm right.

Verse 4

BURKE:	So look out for your own end.
HARE:	Admit it now don't pretend.
BURKE:	I'm warning you.
HARE:	I'm scorning you.
HARE:	I'm right.
BURKE:	You're wrong.
HARE:	You're wrong.
BURKE:	I'm right.

Chorus 2

BOTH:	You, never really knew me,
BURKE:	Now that you do, what do you think?
HARE:	I think you stink.
BURKE:	And so do you.
BOTH:	You, never could see through me.
HARE:	Now that you do, what do you see?
BURKE:	I should've had a guarantee.

Middle 2

HARE:	For you I've got some information,
	I'd have let you walk the streets in my moonlight.
BURKE:	I'll take my leave for some new destination.
	Burke and Hare we will be history tonight.
HARE:	I must've been an idiot to come with you this far.
	I've burned my fingers all because of you.
BURKE:	Now when I look into the future I'm the wasp and you're the jar.
	I'll swing my sting and wing it from the zoo.

Verse 5

HARE:	Your attitude is crazy.
BURKE:	Your memory is hazy.
HARE:	I trusted you.
BURKE:	I'm watching you.
HARE:	I'm right.
BURKE:	You're wrong.
HARE:	You're wrong

BURKE:	I'm right.

Verse 6

HARE:	I'm right.
BURKE:	You're wrong.
HARE:	You're wrong
BURKE:	I'm right.
HARE:	I'm right.
BURKE:	You're wrong.
HARE:	You're wrong
BURKE:	I'm right.
BOTH:	I'm right.
	You're wrong.
	I'm right!

(At the end of the song BURKE has knocked HARE to the ground. There is a loud banging at the front door.)

BURKE: *(Holding the cushion that he has just taken from HARE)* Answer that, and I'll put this out of harms way.

HARE: *(Opening the door)* Maggie! What's up?

MAGGIE: They're on to us! Gray found the M.P.

NELL :He bolted down the street shouting for the police!

MAGGIE: *(Noticing BURKE with cushion)* You and your smart ideas Burke. Leave her alone! The last thing we need now is another corpse.

(Sound of sirens)

NELL: There must be a fire somewhere!

HARE: Lock the door! *(He hides behind the bar.)*

(MRS GRAY wakens and starts screaming.)

BURKE: Calm down, calm down, it's all right...

HARE: *(Keeking over)* Shut her up and we'll kid on that we're not in!

(Thumping begins at the front door.)

MAGGIE: Nell, get upstairs quick and hide the body!

NELL: Again?

MAGGIE: Go!

(NELL exits upstairs.)

MAGGIE: Willie, when I give the word, open the

door.

(HARE goes to the kitchen door. MAGGIE picks up a bottle from behind the bar.)

MAGGIE: Not that one!

(HARE moves. MRS GRAY bites BURKE'S finger.)

BURKE: Ow!

MRS GRAY: Help!

MAGGIE: Ready?

HARE: Ready.

MAGGIE: Now!

(HARE opens the door, GRAY runs in with POLICEMAN and CONSTABLE OUTSIDE.)

MAGGIE: *(At BURKE)* Leave her alone!

(She hits BURKE with the bottle, knocking him out.)

MAGGIE: Thank God you got here in time. He was just about to murder another one!

POLICEMAN: *(Putting the cuffs on BURKE)* So, Mr Burke, we finally caught you. Now, I must warn you that anything you say will be taken down, changed, edited and used against you.

MAGGIE: Don't forget his accomplice, officer.

HARE: Accomplice?

POLICEMAN: Accomplice? Who? *(Approaching HARE, who backs off.)*

MAGGIE: No, not him. She's upstairs.

(CONSTABLE OUTSIDE goes upstairs to get NELL and brings her back.)

POLICEMAN: Also Mr Burke you will be taken to a damp police cell and beaten senseless until you sign a confession. Or you may chose to sign this one that I prepared earlier. *(He blows his whistle)* This court is now in session! All rise for his most exalted highness, Lord Rambo Pickles of Geneva.

Account No.12296475.

(The hotel becomes a court, BURKE and NELL stand behind the bar between the two policemen. Remaining cast become Jurors)

JUDGE: Mr William Burke. Fortunately for our overcrowded prison service and unfortunately for you, yesterdays annual commons vote to introduce hanging, was finally passed. Since capital punishment is now an available option to this court, I must pronounce the harshest penalty open to me ... twenty five pounds fine! Just kidding Mr Burke! You shall be taken from here to a place of execution and hanged by the neck until you are dead. Your corpse will then be given over to the medical school where it should be publicly dissected and anatomised. And may god have mercy on your soul. *(Bangs gavel)* Oh, and Mr Burke ... Have a nice death!

Music-HAVE A NICE DEATH

ALL:
Have a nice death, have a nice death,
You started out with nothing and you've nothing less.
Have a nice death, have a nice death,
All you did was eat and sleep and waste your breath.

You lived your life so lonely, you never had a friend.
No one to cry a tear for you when coming to the end.
You're feeling sorry for yourself, don't feel so sorry for yourself.
You lived your life in misery, you never raised a smile.
You'd like to have been happy but you never had the style.
You're feeling sorry for yourself, don't feel so sorry for yourself.
You're feeling sorry for yourself, stop feeling sorry for yourself.
So have a nice death!

BOOM BOOM!

The Return of Burke and Hare theme

Creepy

Have a nice death

Mr Burke and Mr Hare

Polka

I'm Mis-ter Burke I'm Mis-ter Hare I'm o-ver here he's o-ver there and when we meet you have a per-fect pair _____ for ev'-ry-thing we see we like to share I'm Mis-ter (INST.) When

Slower

I was down and out of luck I did'nt have a pe-ny— I came and split my cash in half although I had'nt a-ny— When I was hun-gry out of bread I did-nt have a far-thing— Fif-ty fif-ty's what I said and then we both were star-ving— (INST.) I'm Mis-ter In case your bo-dy dis-a-ppears in-to thin air—

147

Bodysnatching baby

doc-tor for the will (INST.)

Dal $ | Coda

I'm his | Com-fort fun mo-ney on the vein is the

quest of my suc-cess se-cu-ri-ty laughs cash o-ver-drafts won't

let me get de-pressed Se-ttle down smile take it ea-sy vein a mile is the

goal in-side my mind so we mur-der catch suff-o-cate snatch for the

be-ne-fit of man-kind So we mur-der catch suff-o-cate snatch

mur-der catch suff-o-cate snatch mur-der catch suff-o-cate snatch for the

be-ne-fit of man-kind

Mr Gray's happy days

What's that you say Mister Gray? Things will be o. k. to-day if

ev-ry-bo-dy smiles they will be hap-py —

Mis-ter Gray what's that you say? I can live the Bri-tish way

I'm your ave-rage rich suc-cess-ful chap-pie   you

try to tell me that there's un-em-ploy-ment (un-em-ploy-ment) It's

not my fault I did-int sack them all (He did-int sack us all) I

ne-ver let it spoil my own en – joy-ment (His en-joy-ment) I

simp-ly slide my card in-to the wall (And grab some mo-ney) Lots and

lots of love-ly mo-ney (And grab some mo-ney) Lots and

lots of love-ly cash Hey! cave — Be-cause we

won't be there What's that you say Mis-ter Gray?

Things will be o.k. to-day if ev-'ry-bo-dy smiles they will be

hap-py — Mis-ter Gray what's that you say?

I can live the British way I'm your ave-rage rich suc-cess-ful chap-pie

151

Transplant surgery

G chord vamp until voice starts

freely

If you've got to crack an egg to make an om-lette or kill a man to give a dog a bone and the world is bet-ter for it, let so-ci-e-ty ig-nore it, if it's some-bo-dy or some-thing they don't own

We

dear

GETTING FASTER...

One more life won't make a speck of diff'-rence as a sac-ri-fice to save a hun-dred more and a hun-dred more than e-ven up the score

Trans-plant sur-ger-y trans-plant sur-ger-y

trans-plant sur-ger-y's what it's all a-bout

Trans-plant sur-ger-y's what it's all a-bout we've

been ning the pop-u-la-tion in me-di-cine's fin-al bout If you

want to put the kid-neys in you've got to take them out

Trans-plant sur-ger-y's what it's all a-bout

Hearts lungs li-ver and kid-neys

hair u-pon your head

Skin graft e-mer-gen-cy to stop you be-ing

dead

Front-al lo-bo-to-my spare parts are brought to me I'll

e-ven swap your eyes I get a

taste of waste when a-ny-bo-dy

dies— Trans-plant sur-ger-y Trans-plant sur-ger-y

Trans-plant sur-ger-y's what it's all a-bout

First you will

some-times you change your mind and that just drives me
mad Ev'-ry night I stand out-side your
house in soak-ing rain You tell me to come in —
— and then you change your mind a-gain —
I could wait for years you know but ba-by can't you
see we could start a-gain right now if
you would just a-gree fall in love with me ba-by can't you
see Oh how hap-py we would be if you fell in love with me

Your attitude is crazy

A selected list of
dualchas
publications